JUDO
ROAD TO CHAMPION

Timo Korpiola

JUDO
ROAD TO CHAMPION

Assistant and photos

Peter Mickelsson

Photographs by: Peter Mickelsson, except for photos on pages 182-189.
Editor and photo editor: Jorma Paasi; Original layout: Jukka Iivarinen / Vitale Ay

Publisher: BoD · Books on Demand, Mannerheimintie 12 B, 00100 Helsinki, bod@bod.fi
Printed by: Libri Plureos GmbH, Friedensallee 273, 22763 Hamburg, Germany

ISBN: 978-952-80-8388-7

Contents

KATAME-WAZA – CONTROL TECHNIQUES

Forewords

JUDO – ROAD TO CHAMPION

- ▶ This book gives the judoka and judo coach a basic overview of what and
  how to do to reach the top level of international judo.

- ▶ It guides the judoka, once the basic techniques have been mastered, to find his/her own personal versatility in judo.

- ▶ The book includes an analysis of past Olympic champions and judo champions of recent decades, including Kosei
  Inoue, Udo Qellmalz, Jeon Ki-Young, Toshihiko Koga and Mark Huizinga; what qualities they have been required to
  have and how they have trained judo to achieve their goals and what their favourite moves have been in competition.

- ▶ Most of the ippons done in competitions are still done using pure basic techniques – the in-
  genious judo developed by Jigoro Kano has not changed in essence over time.

- ▶ Judo techniques presented in this book are a collection of some 1,000 ippons and other
  effective techniques used to win matches in international competitions in the 21st century.

- ▶ It contains most of the techniques used in all judo competitions today.

- ▶ The most important judo throws most commonly used in competition are
  extensively covered, and control techniques used in judo competitions.

- ▶ It deals extensively with the transition from judo throws to hold downs, armlocks and chokes.

- ▶ Instructions and examples of the tokui-waza system required of an international level competitor are given.

- ▶ A reference book for every judo coach, teacher and judoka aiming for the top international level.

Helsinki, October 2014 and September 2024

Timo Korpiola, Kodokan 6th dan

DEDICATION AND ACKNOWLEDGEMENTS

The book is dedicated to my wife Orvokki. Without her support during my judo career of more than half a century and her understanding and long-suffering while making this book, the work would never have come into being. She has also been a great discussion partner throughout the long book project.

The foundation for my judo was given to me by Ichiro Abe, 10th dan. His message about the importance and significance of learning the complete basic technique in judo has been a guiding principle throughout my judo career. This message has always been passed on to me, including in this book. My most important judo teachers and examples in my life are also 10th dan Toshiro Daigo and Anton Geesink. The latter's aphorism "a champion must look like a champion" has been permanently in my mind for more than four decades. Daigo's judo skills and his discretion and hospitality are second to none. I feel a great sense of gratitude towards the above masters.

This is an opportunity to thank all the judoka with whom I have had the privilege of practising judo. Special thanks go to Peter Mickelsson, with whom I have worked through the techniques in this book over the past few years. Peter did a tremendous amount of shooting photos for the book and he has helped me in many other ways in the making of the book. The techniques are also presented by my long-time judo friends Vesa Riihelä and Tomi Nurminen. They devoted themselves to their task with great dedication and did an excellent job. My sincere thanks go to them. My thanks also go to the judokas not mentioned here who have helped me with the book.

My brother Kyösti, 7th dan, with whom I have been practising throughout my judo career, also consulted the manuscript. I thank him for his advice and for the years of judo together.

Requirements to Become a Judo Champion

THE MENTAL QUALITIES REQUIRED

- The ability and willingness to dedicate oneself to judo, not 90–95%, but 100%.
- The will to win, the passion for perfect performances – this is ippon.
- Determination, diligence and perseverance towards goals and dreams.
- Ambition, enthusiasm to train harder than your competitors.
- Respect for other judokas.
- The humility to listen to and learn from old masters and teachers.
- Self-confidence and the courage to take risks.
- Insight and belief in oneself and one's own abilities.
- The ability to analyse, understand and improve one's own judo and to create a judo strategy that suits oneself.
- Love for the sport.

Jouni Korkka and Pasi Oinas perform Kime no Kata, which requires good concentration.

JUDO SKILLS

- ▶ Master the basics of judo, such as grip, breaking the balance, feint and movement.
- ▶ Master nage-waza (throws) and katame-waza (control techniques) on both sides.
- ▶ Know variations to your tokui-waza (favourite moves) and the situations in which they are performed.
- ▶ Create a tokui-waza system that suits you and can be used effectively in all situations and against all types of opponents.
- ▶ Be able to compete (shiai) and, in this context, be able to formulate tactics for each match.
- ▶ Know nage-no-kata and katame-no-kata.

Neil Adams, currently 9th dan, teaching juji-gatame at the Järvenpää camp in March 2008.

Learning to Become a Judo Champion

UKEMI (THE ART OF FALLING)

Introduction

- ▶ Ukemi is an essential part of the fantastic judo developed by Jigoro Kano.
- ▶ With ukemi, falling from throws is safe.
- ▶ Ukemi is a good warm-up at the beginning of each exercise.
- ▶ Ukemi is essential to learn. It eliminates the fear of falling, which would other-wise prevent proper practicing of throwing.
- ▶ Learning ukemi starts as a solo exercise.

Technique

The following examples of ukemi practice are done with a partner in a frequently repeated competitive situation. At the point when uke is rising from a kneeling position with one knee in front, tori unbalances uke's already poor balance and easily throws uke. Throws are made with uke as low as possible. Throws are made on both sides.

Ukemi backward and to the side

O-soto-gari

Ko-soto-gari

Uchi-mata, can be done on either of uke's legs

Ukemi by standing up, te-waza by releasing grip

Ukemi staying on the mat, yoko-tomoe-nage

THROWING – UKEMI – GOING TO THE MAT
PREVENTING GOING TO THE MAT – TURNING – HOLD DOWN

The throw – going to the mat – chained exercise includes several drills important for the competitor.
- Throwing utilising uke's sloppy landing to the mat.
- Ukemi.
- Moving to the mat after the throw, hold down (or juji-gatame, for example).
- Escape from the control technique.
- Avoiding a full ippon on the way down.
- Preventing a tie-up (or armlock).
- Turning (when tori is on his back on the mat).
- Hold down.

Tai-otoshi – kesa-gatame (can also be any other throw or hold down) – escape from hold down

Blocking uke's entry after the throw (here tai-otoshi) into the hold down – "bear hug turn" – hold down (here tate-shiho-gatame)

Introduction

▶ Judo throws are usually executed from movement, which is why good stance and
correct movement are important for attack, defence and balance.
▶ All judo throws are started with tai-sabaki, ayumi-ashi or tsugi-ashi.
▶ A variety of movement exercises alone and with a partner are essential for all judokas.
▶ The importance of shisei and shintai training for judoka is comparable to the
importance of movement and step pattern training for competitive dancers.

Shisei, posture

A good judo stance is relaxed but alert. The feet are firmly but flexibly
on the ground at shoulder-width. The back is straight.

Natural posture,
shizen-hontai

Natural stance right or left foot
in front, migi or hidari shizentai

Defensive stance, right or left, foot
in front, migi or hidari jigotai

Shintai, movement ("a piece of silk paper between the heel and the tatami")

Ayumi-ashi – sliding alternating walk

▶ Ayumi-ashi should be practised continuously with a variety of rhythm
changes, jumping, moving forward and backward.
▶ Ayumi-ashi is based on backward throws as uke moves backward or forward, including o-soto-gari and ko-uchi-gari.
▶ Good control of the ayumi-ashi is essential for tai-sabaki.

← back   ayumi-ashi   forward →

Example of ayumi-ashi movement

Entering o-soto-gari

Tsugi-ashi – moving one foot in front

- ▸ Tsugi-ashi should be practised in a variety of ways, right and left, alternating rhythm, jumping, moving in all directions: forward, backward, sideways and in a circle.
- ▸ The tsugi-ashi is based on backward throws such as the o-uchi-gari, ko-uchi-gari and ko-soto-gari.
- ▸ The comprehensive skill of the tsugi-ashi is essential for the tai-sabaki.

Example of tsugi-ashi movement

Entering tomoe-nage, tori advancing with tsugi-ashi.

- Throws are started with a turn or ayumi-ashi or tsugi-ashi combined with a turn.
- Repetitions of the various turns should be performed with each exercise in order to make them reflex-like and fast.
- When performing throws, the steps of tai-sabaki are of different lengths and rhythms. For example, when stepping forward in the uchi-mata, the 180 degree tai-sabaki is performed almost from a standing position, see page 131.
- Tai-sabaki exercises are always performed on both sides.

Tai-sabaki backwards

Tai-sabaki on hidari 45 degrees (right foot back)	Tai-sabaki on hidari 90 degrees (right foot back)	Tai-sabaki on migi 90 + 90 degrees (left – right foot)	Tai-sabaki on migi 180 degrees (left foot back)

Application to throws:
- 45 degrees including ko-uchi-gari, de-ashi-harai, first step for many throws and blocking throws.
- 90 degrees, including de-ashi-harai, first step for multiple throws, blocking throws.
- 90 + 90 degrees forward throws.
- 180 degree forward throws.

Tai-sabaki forward

Tai-sabaki on migi
45 + 90 + 45 degrees

Tai-sabaki on migi
90 + 90 degrees

Tai-sabaki on migi
180 degrees

See page 86, tsurikomi-goshi

Tori's turn to the side

Introduction

- A judoka must have a good command of a wide range of hand grips.
- Good posture, grip and correct movement create the conditions for judo throws.
- The grip is used to make throws, to control space and to control the opponent.
- One's favourite movements must be able to be performed with different grips.
- Tori must know which grip is the most advantageous to throw with, for example, the tsurite grip (lapel grip) for several ashi-wazas.
- Tori must 1. Get his favourite grip, or 2. Counter uke's attempt to take a grip and then take his own grip, or 3. If uke has got his favourite grip, break it and take his own grip.
- Once the desired grip has been obtained from uke, immediate efforts must be made to use it for your own moves.
- Grips must be taken into account in all exercises.
- The grip must be firm but at the same time flexible.
- Moving the wrist releases the elbow and shoulder for the throw.
- Tori must try to prevent the opponent from getting a two-handed grip and try to attack just when the opponent has only a one-handed grip.

Technique

Basic grip

- The term hikite describes a grip on an opponent's sleeve, the pulling hand.
- The term tsurite describes a grip on the opponent's collar, the power and lifting hand.
- In the basic grip, the left hand grabs uke's right sleeve above the elbow and the right hand grabs uke's lapel below the left collarbone.
- The basic grip is the most effective grip in judo, both in attack and defence.
- For example, one hand on the neck, cannot effectively unbalance uke backwards and it is also bad for defence.
- In ai-yotsu, both fighters have the same sided grip. In kenka-yotsu, one has a migi and the other a hidari grip.

Ai-yotsu

Kenka-yotsu

Different grips

Depending on the tactics, competitors must be able to perform their favourite moves using **several different grips**.

▶ The grip can be from the back, lapel, back of the neck, down on the sleeve and almost anywhere on the opponent's judogi, belt or above the belt.

▶ The competition rules set limitations on taking grip below the belt in standing judo. It is also forbidden to take hold of the inside of the opponent's sleeve.

▶ Grabbing the belt requires an immediate attack.

▶ In competitions, the **same-sided grips** on the cuff, the sleeve with both hands, the sleeve and the same-sided collar and the belt, which are useful as such, require immediate attack.

▶ **One-handed grips** are used in competitions, for example, in the starting position, for the following throws: o-soto-gari, de-ashi-harai from the front and back of the step of uke, o-uchi-gari, ko-uchi-gari, sode-tsurikomi-goshi and seoi-nage.

O-uchi-gari   Sode-tsurikomi-goshi   De-ashi-harai

Ways to get a grip:

▶ Be faster than your opponent.
▶ Distract the opponent, for example, with a hand movement, such as an open palm
  in front of his face and take your own grip quickly, see pictures below.

▶ Take advantage of your own and your opponent's movement.
▶ Passing the grip: the left hand grabs uke's left lapel and passes it to the right hand. Tori pulls or
  pushes uke and at the same time grabs uke's right sleeve with the left hand, pictures below.

▶ Using the body to get a grip.

From this situation, one can attack backwards with the o-soto-gari and o-uchi-
gari and forwards with all the so-called big throws forward.

Preventing uke from getting a grip

▶ Block with the hand opponent's attempt to get a grip and immediately take your own grip.
▶ Do not let uke get close.
▶ Go around the opponent.

Breaking the grip

▶ Release the grip with the hand without the help of the other hand using body strength.
▶ Make your own throwing attempt.

Introduction

- Tsukuri is defined below as tori's preparation for the throw prior to the kuzushi.
- The kuzushi is used to break uke's balance so that tori can effectively attack without fear of a counter-attack by uke.
- With tsukuri, uke is temporarily, "frozen", an opportunity which tori utilises, i.e. tori's action, uke's reaction, tori's opening, kuzushi, the entry and the throw.
- In tsukuri, tori's whole body is involved, even if the actual action is performed with only one part of the body, such as hands, feet or hands and feet.
- Tsukuri should be included in all throwing practice, for example in uchi-komi.
- What enables the throw is as important as the throw itself.

Technique

- The following are commonly used preparatory actions (tsukuri) for the throws.

Feinting with hands and upper body

Push down – push to the back or pull to the front	Pull forward – push back	Push back – pull forward	Pull to the side – pull to the opposite side diagonally to the front or to the side

Pushing the hand to the side in front of uke's body – kuzushi Pushing and pulling back and forth with the hands Lifting and pushing down with the hands

Feinting with feet and lower body

Lifting the knee up – return – attack

Stepping forward – return – attack

Kneeling – dropping the body down

Stepping with feet in different directions

Feinting with hands and feet

Stepping forward – pushing
with hands – pulling
forward

Kuzushi and foot to hidari –
turn – throw to migi side

Straight lift up with hands
and body, stepping forward

Three types of combinations

1. Feint combination
(for example with o-uchi-gari)

2. Follow-up combination, throwing
attempt with for example ko-soto-
gari and continuing with another throw

3. Separate throws
combination, attempt –
return – attack

Introduction

▶ Tori breaks uke's balance so that uke cannot attack and tori can safely continue the throw.
▶ Kuzushi is initially done with the hands, followed by the whole body.
▶ Depending on the throw, the direction of the kuzushi varies.
▶ The direction of the kuzushi of the throw varies greatly with variations of it and with different situations.
▶ Kuzushi should be practised regularly, alone and with a partner. When practising alone,
   you should also use aids to strengthen your kuzushi, such as resistance bands.

Technique

▶ The following are the basic kuzushi directions for some throws to the right (migi).

To the back left
o-soto-gari

To the back
ko-soto-gake (tani-otoshi)

To the left side
yoko-otoshi

To the front right
harai-goshi

Forward
tomoe-nage

To the back right,
o-uchi-gari

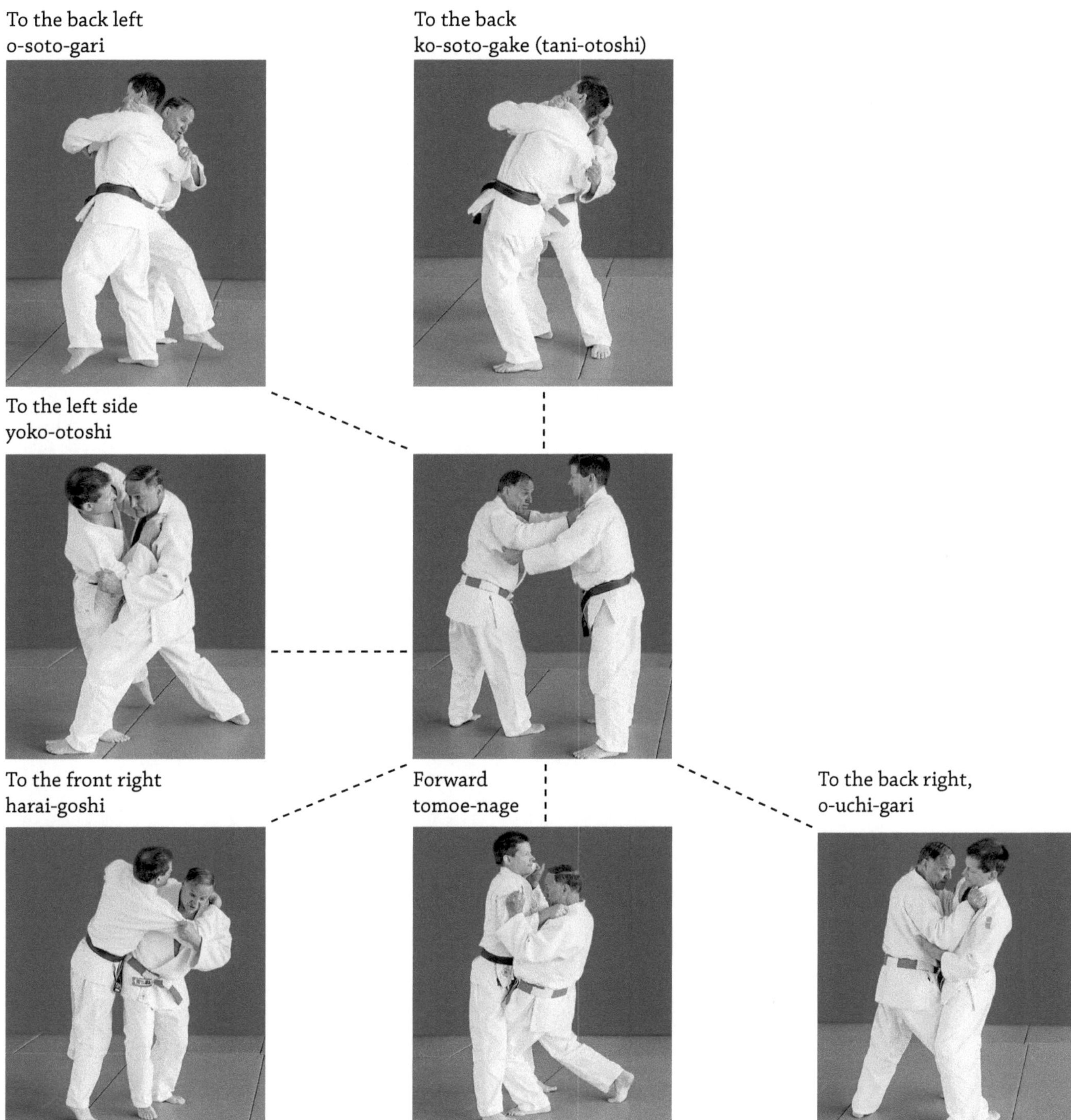

Introduction

▶ Tandoku-renshu is one of the three main forms of judo training, along with uchi-komi and randori.
▶ Tens of thousands of repetitions are required to learn judo movements effectively. One Japanese champion used to do ten thousand repetitions a day with ashi-waza before major competitions!
▶ Tokui-waza throw(s) should be repeated from one hundred to four hundred times a day.
▶ Individual practice is important for every judoka to learn step patterns, to gain rhythm, speed and judo power, and to maintain judo skills.
▶ An effective tandoku-renshu practice, for example, done at home, takes 1–2 hours.

Technique

Tandoku-renshu without aids

▶ The solo training programme should be varied. It should include judo movements (ayumi-ashi and tsugi-ashi) and turns (tai-sabaki) in various forms, as well as judo throws and control movements.
▶ The movements are performed on both sides.
▶ Rhythmic music is suitable for solo practice.

Programme

▶ Judo movements, ayumi-ashi and tsugi-ashi with slow, fast rhythm variations, jumping, changing directions, etc. See pages 18–19.
▶ Tai-sabaki, 10 repetitions of each form. See pages 20–21.
▶ Throws, 10–20 repetitions of each. The most important throws for oneself, performed in several ways.
▶ Harais = (barais): de-ashi-harai, okuri-ashi-harai, harai-tsurikomi-ashi plus hiza-guruma and sasae-tsurikomi-ashi.

▶ Gari throws: o-soto-gari, o-uchi-gari, ko-uchi-gari, ko-soto-gari with ko-soto-gake.

▶ Throws with two supporting legs: tsurikomi-goshi with different steps, see page
  86, o-goshi, koshi-guruma, seoi-nage throws and tai-otoshi.

▶ Single support leg throws: uchi-mata, harai-goshi, ashi-guruma, etc.

▶ Sutemi-waza throws: tomoe-nage, ura-nage and tani-otoshi.

▶ **Daily practice of tokui-waza:** basic throwing, variations and combinations from various situations with
  combinations to the back with the second tokui-waza, going to the mat to take the favourite katame-waza.
▶ Kumikata, blocking and counter-throws.

Tandoku-renshu with aids

With weight vests

  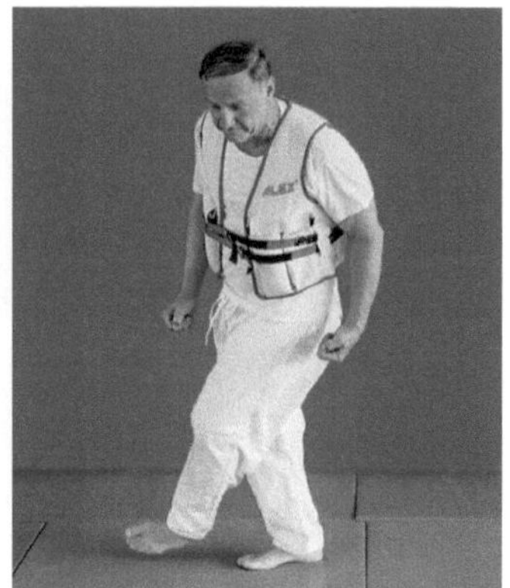

With hand and ankle weights

Performing resistance band pulls with both hands.

 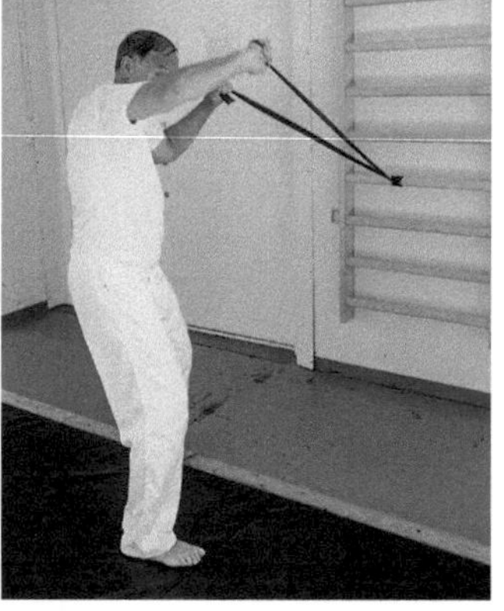 

Hikite   Tsurite

 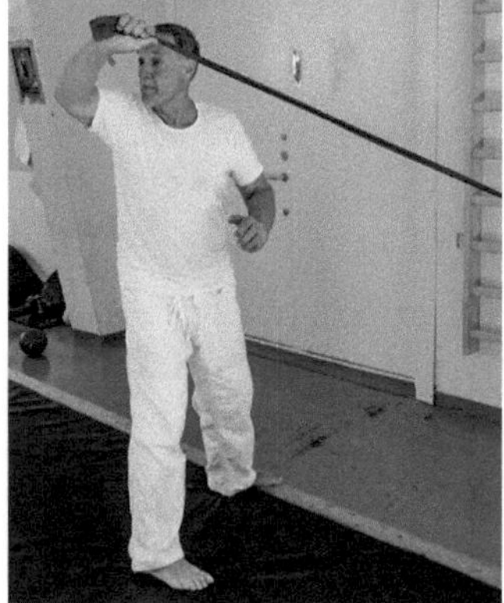  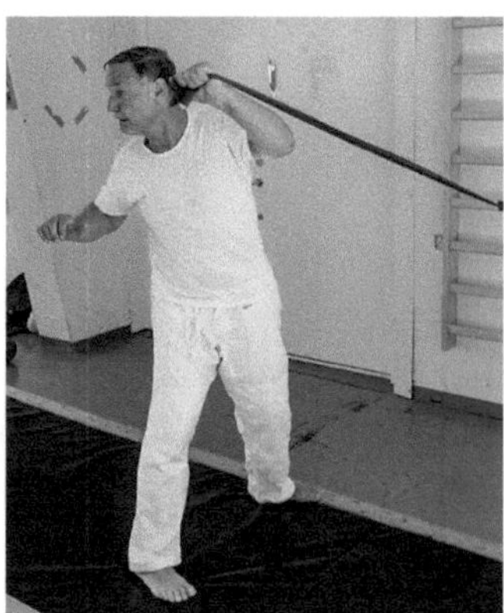

With bands or belt

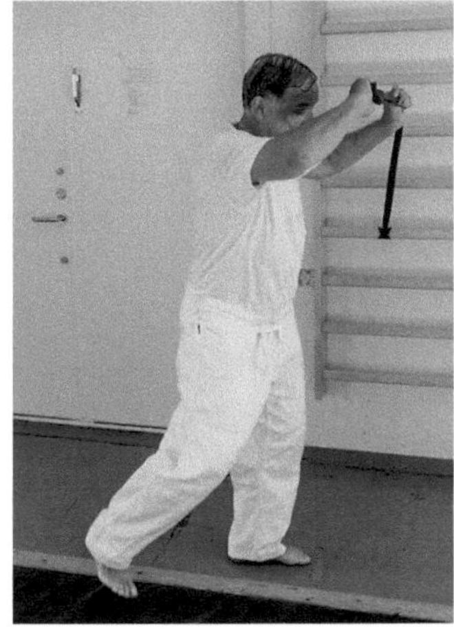  

Isometric training with the belt.

▶ Finally, hold the movement for 6–12
  seconds at maximum force.

Examples of bag training
▶ The weight of the bag varies considerably depending on the exercise, at least 10% of your own weight.

Arm flexor exercise   Over the shoulder rotation in both directions

Introduction

- ▶ Uchi-komi with tandoku-renshu and randori are the most important forms of training in judo.
- ▶ Uchi-komi is the **best way** to gain judo power, stamina, endurance and speed.
- ▶ Uchi-komi requires total concentration throughout the training, both from uke and tori.
- ▶ In uchi-komi, the judo move, throw or katame-waza is always repeated carefully and in the same way.
- ▶ In uchi-komi, the strength of the whole body is used.
- ▶ In uchi-komi you can also practise the different phases of the movement.
- ▶ Before the exercise, the position, resistance, the number of repetitions, etc. are agreed with the partner.

Technique

- ▶ An uchi-komi exercise can last from a few minutes up to **two hours**.
- ▶ In traditional uchi-komi, a series of 10–30 repetitions are made in turn.
- ▶ When building stamina or judo power, the repetitions are structured in a pyramid, for example 10–20–30–20–10 repetitions or descending 30–20–10 repetitions.
- ▶ One does the whole set and the other rests between sets.
- ▶ The resistance is set according to the goal.
- ▶ The sets always end with a throw.

Stationary uchi-komi

Basic stance

Tsukuri

Opening

Kuzushi

Entry

Throw before the kake phase.

Return to basic stance.

Uchi-komi in motion

- ▶ Uke steps forward, sideways or backwards. After each uchi-komi, uke and tori return to the starting stance.
- ▶ The sequence can be done in such a way that there are 10 to 20 repetitions.
- ▶ The uchi-komi series can be built up by doing the same throw forward-sideways-back in turn and repeating this five times, making 15 repetitions for the whole series.
- ▶ Uchi-komi should include: tsukuri – opening – kuzushi – entering.

Uchi-komi when uke steps forward

Uchi-komi with tori's turn when uke steps to the side

Uchi-komi when uke steps backwards

Three person uchi-komi (power uchi-komi)

Uchi-komi changing the throw

(”The one holding uke's belt is standing or sitting”).

▶ Five repetitions at
  full speed. Hold for
  about 2–3 seconds.

▶ Two combination throws in turn.
▶ The throws can be done in turn after turn or depending on
  how uke reacts to the throw.
▶ In tai-otoshi – o-uchi-gari training, tori's 1st and 2nd steps
  are the same for both throws.

Uchi-komi uke squatting

Pulling hand, hikite – uchi-komi

Lifting hand, tsurite – uchi-komi

NAGE-KOMI – THROWING EXERCISE

▶ When practising throwing, always make sure that the rhythm is correct first. After that, comes speed and power.
▶ The final stage of the throw, the kake, is learned by completing the throw.
▶ It is not essential for throwing to practice that the throw is made quickly. What is important is that the throw is made at the right time and correctly.
▶ The role of uke is important when practising throwing. Under no circumstances should uke jump for ukemi.
▶ Requires a good throwing mat, in some exercises a soft mat.

The impact point ("explosion")

In the throw, uke concentrates all his mental and physical energy at a single point of contact, for example, hip, upper arm, leg, through which all uke's energy is discharged to complete the throw. The end result is an IPPON.

Harai-goshi – hip sweep (impact point on the hip)

Throwing Stages:

| tsukuri | opening kuzushi | contact point | kake, that is, completion of the throw. |

Throwing practice in a group

▶ The group consists of six judokas. Each in turn throws five times each. There will be 25 throws for each of them.

Throwing practice in a group

▶ The group consists of six judokas. One judoka throws each of them once with explosive force on a soft mat.

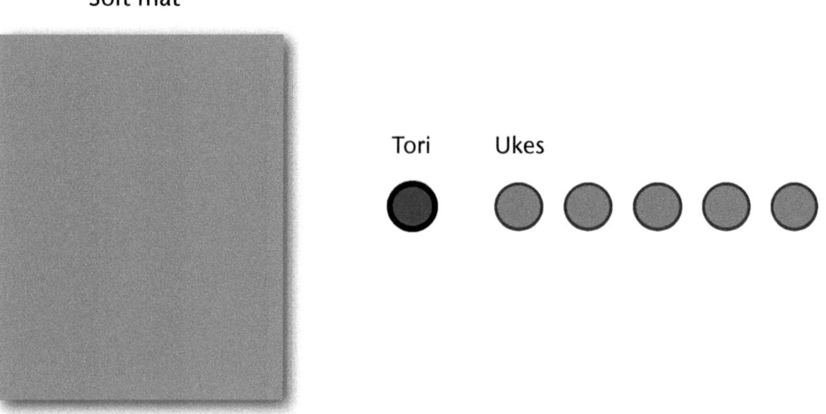

Isometric throwing exercise with letting loose

▶ A third person holds the throw from the belt for about five seconds, then releases the grip on the belt. This exercise develops acceleration in particular.

YAKU-SOKU-GEIKO – PRE-ARRANGED PAIR TRAINING

- ▶ Pair training in motion without a deliberately completed throw.
- ▶ Before the exercise, it is agreed which movements will be practised and how. For example, you can agree to practice all throws, some throws, or just one throw.
- ▶ Uke does not fight back when tori makes the throws, but moves naturally.
- ▶ Tori makes each throw **timely right** and **100% correct**.
- ▶ A demanding form of exercise that requires full concentration from both parties.

The author and Vesa Riihelä practising the kakari-geiko

KAKARI-GEIKO – ATTACK EXERCISE WITH A PARTNER

- ▶ Before the exercise, it is agreed which moves will be practised and how the exercise will be carried out. For example, the duration of the exercise and whether the exercise will be done with all or a single throw.
- ▶ A form of exercise in which tori and uke perform the movements to the full. Tori will constantly try to throw uke and uke will counter the throwing attempts by defending himself with something other than his hands.
- ▶ Counter-throwing is allowed when tori's throwing attempt is poor.
- ▶ A **difficult and demanding form of training** which requires advanced judo skills on both sides.
- ▶ A difficult form of training which develops the mental qualities of the practitioners in particular.

RANDORI – COMPETITION-LIKE TRAINING

- The most important form of studying, learning and practising judo.
- Very often the aim of randori is **misunderstood**.
- What good is a five-minute randori for a competitor if all that happens is standing stiffly and resisting?
- All judokas, regardless of age or gender, can do randori.
- In a competition (shiai), the aim is to win, in randori there are no points and **there is no winner and loser**. In fact, the winner is the one who has learned the most from the randori.
- Randori is judo learning at its best. It's about developing what you already know and learning what you don't yet know.
- The resistance should be 50–60% of the maximum. Harder resistance is not conducive to creative skill development and experimentation.

Randori at the big dojo in Kodokan

SHIAI – COMPETITION

Competition event and competition is an essential and important part of judo.

Before the matches

- Preparation is a personal experience for each competitor.
- Success requires good mental and physical preparation from everyone.
- **For each match and each competitor, a tactic must be defined** and followed during the match.
- On the day of the match, a good warm-up of about one hour, including gymnastics, tandoku renshu, uchi-komi and possibly light randori.
- Pre-match warm-up of about fifteen minutes.
- Before entering the tatami, you must signal to your opponent who the winner is, i.e. "the winner must look like the winner".

During the match

▶ Stick to the match tactics planned beforehand.
▶ Go into the match with only **victory in mind**, even if you are not the favourite to win.
▶ Keep the initiative in your own hands from the start of the match.
▶ Prevent your opponent from getting a good grip.
▶ Break your opponent's grip if he has already got it.
▶ Maintain aggressive judo, i.e. feet, hands and body in motion at all times, trying to find a solution continuously.
▶ Keeping distance from the opponent, turning in the opposite direction and distracting the opponent so that the opponent cannot recover.
▶ Aim to win with an ippon, because only then can you be sure of winning.
▶ Remember that the last few seconds are the time to win or lose.
▶ When you are losing, you must not rush. You have to keep a cool head until the end.

Shiai at the 2008 Finnish Open

After a match or matches

▶ After winning a match, get your mind and body back ready for the next match.
▶ The analysis of the competitions will only take place in the following days.
▶ You must be happy about your victories, but remember to **keep an open and humble mind**.
▶ A defeat is not a disaster for anyone – it's a **learning experience**.

Introduction

▶ A competition career at the top usually lasts between 4 and 8 years. The current points system means that the top players meet each other very often. To get wins against the same opponents, a top judoka has to have something new for every major competition.

▶ Many champions during their careers have scored **ippons** in international competitions with **15–20 different techniques**.

▶ Some champions have won Olympic gold or world titles by winning all their matches with different techniques.

▶ A top class judoka must be **versatile** and have a **wide range of favourite movement system**. Every opponent is different and almost all judo techniques are used to win international competitions.

▶ The broader and more comprehensive your favourite movement system is, the better your chances are for success.

▶ Building a tokui-waza system should begin after you have a good command of the basic techniques of judo on both sides.

▶ The tokui-waza system is **logically constructed** from different types of throws and control techniques.

▶ A strategic decision needs to be taken on how much to focus on nage-waza and katame-waza.

Techniques

▶ First you have to decide which side will be the main throwing side, i.e. whether it will be migi or hidari. This is often a natural choice.

▶ The tokui-waza system is usually built **around** a so-called ”**big throw**” forward. Major throws include uchi-mata, seoi-nage throws, harai-goshi, koshi-guruma and tai-otoshi.

▶ The first tokui-waza must be mastered in all possible situations, regardless of whether the opponent has a migi or a hidari grip.

▶ **The second tokui-waza** is usually one of the leg throws backwards, such as o-uchi-gari or ko-uchi-gari. It should form another part of the combination with the first tokui-waza.

▶ Tokui-waza also includes big or small throws to the other side.

▶ De-ashi-harai is a natural part of most competitors' tokui-waza systems.

▶ A good system also includes counter-throws, often sutemi-wazas such as tomoe-nage, ura-nage and tani-otoshi, which also complement the system because they are downward throws.

▶ Around the first tokui-waza, other throws of the same type should also be practised, such as harai-goshi and ashi-guruma together with uchi-mata.

▶ A good favourite movement system also includes strong mat judo so that you never lose on the mat, as well as one must be able to score an ippon with a favourite hold down, armlock or choke.

AN EXAMPLE OF A TOKUI WAZA SYSTEM BUILT AROUND MIGI UCHI-MATA

O-soto-gari
(Ko-uchi-gari)

Ko-soto-gake
(Tani-otoshi)

O-uchi-gari

De-ashi-harai

Hidari de-ashi-harai, ko-soto-gari, okuri-ashi-harai

Uchi-mata
(harai-goshi, ashi-guruma)

Okuri-eri-jime/koshi-jime

Ko-uchi-gari
(O-soto-gari)
Ura-nage/Tani-otoshi
O-uchi-gari
De-ashi-harai
Okuri-ashi-harai
Hidari sode-tsurikomi-goshi,
ippon-seoi-nage,
de-ashi-harai
Ippon-seoi-nage
Tomoe-nage
Yoko-shiho-gatame
Juji-gatame

NAGE-WAZA

DE-ASHI-HARAI · TSUBAME-GAESHI

OKURI-ASHI-HARAI · HARAI-TSURIKOMI-ASHI

SASAE-TSURIKOMI-ASHI · HIZA-GURUMA

NAGE-WAZA (THROWING TECHNIQUES)

DE-ASHI-HARAI – ADVANCING OR FRONT FOOT SWEEP

▶ Uke steps forward with his right foot. At the same time, tori moves to uke's side with a 90-degree backwards tai-sabaki with his right foot. Tori sweeps uke's advancing foot with the sole of his left sole just
before uke's weight shifts onto his right foot. Finally, tori uses his hands to pull uke straight down. In de-
ashi-harai, tori always sweeps uke's foot in front forward. De-ashi-harai requires tori to be relaxed and have
a controlled grip, good timing and the ability to attract uke to step in the way he wants. De-ashi-harai is
often performed with an opposite grip so that tori's left hand is on uke's right lapel above uke's hand.

PREPARATORY ACTIONS (TSUKURI) FOR DE-ASHI-HARAI

▶ In de-ashi-harai, tori signals to uke that there is no danger and thus causes uke to move carelessly. Tori pro-
vokes uke to step as he wishes, for example by pushing, pulling, pushing down or lifting his arm or arms.

VARIATIONS AND SITUATIONS FOR APPLYING DE-ASHI-HARAI

Push-pull de-ashi-harai
▶ Tori uses his right hand and body to push uke firmly backwards, after which tori relaxes
his grip for a moment and, pulling gently, tempts uke to step forward first with his left and
then with his right foot. Tori then sweeps uke's right foot as he steps forward.

Combination migi sasae-tsurikomi-ashi/hiza-guruma – hidari de-ashi-harai

▶ Uke counters tori's sasae-tsurikomi-ashi/hiza-guruma by stepping forward with his left foot, after which tori sweeps uke's left foot with his right foot.

One-handed de-ashi-harai

▶ In the starting position, tori and uke have a one-handed grip. Using a calm retreat and a full body movement tori can cause uke to step forward carelessly with his left foot, or tori can force uke in jigotai stance to step forward with his left foot by pulling hard, giving tori an opportunity to sweep the foot.

Combination feint hidari uchi-mata – migi de-ashi-harai

▶ Tori jumps on his right foot close to uke's right foot as if to do a hidari uchi-mata. Uke counters by stepping forward with his right foot. Tori sweeps with his left foot just as the weight of uke's body is about to shift on his right foot. If the weight of uke's body has already shifted to the right foot, tori makes a ko-soto-gari or ko-soto-gake.

Combination feint hidari o-soto-gari – migi de-ashi-harai

- ▶ Tori makes a feint of hidari o-soto-gari or feints subtly as if going into an o-soto-gari. Uke counters by stepping forward with his right foot. Tori quickly returns to the starting position and sweeps uke's advancing foot with his left foot before the weight of uke's body has shifted to the foot. If uke's balance has already shifted to his right foot, tori does a ko-soto-gari or ko-soto-gake.

De-ashi-harai kaeshi-waza when uke starts to enter for the throw

- ▶ Uke carelessly starts a throwing attempt with his right foot, for example, uchi-mata. Tori senses the situation and sweeps the advancing foot before the weight of uke's body has shifted to it.

De-ashi-harai kaeshi-waza to uke's o-uchi-gari

- ▶ While uke is making an o-uchi-gari throw, tori blocks the throw attempt by straightening his left arm. Before the weight of uke's body has shifted to uke's right foot, tori sweeps it with his left foot.
  Depending on the situation, tori may take a step backwards with his right foot before the sweep.

De-ashi-harai kaeshi-waza when uke returns from a throw attempt

▶ Uke returns from a failed throw attempt, such as a seoi-nage or harai-goshi. Tori sweeps uke's right support leg at the moment when uke is releasing his foot from the ground to return to the original position.

De-ashi-harai variation, tori and uke are facing each other during the throw

▶ Uke steps forward with his right foot. Tori responds with a quick 45 degree right foot retreating tai-sabaki. Before the weight of uke's body has shifted to the advancing foot, tori sweeps it diagonally to the front.

De-ashi-harai in jigotai position

▶ Tori pulls uke sideways or forward to the right while both are in a defensive position. As uke moves his right foot sideways, tori sweeps it with his left foot.

De-ashi-harai variation, moving sideways

▶ Tori follows uke's movement to the right. Tori sweeps uke's right foot forward just as the weight of the body is about to shift to it. During the sweep phase, tori's right foot is at a 45–90 degree angle to uke.

De-ashi-harai variation, as uke retreats

▶ Uke moves backwards. Just as uke's right foot is about to come off the ground, tori enters with ayumi-ashi or tsugi-ashi and sweeps uke's right foot with his left foot diagonally to the front. Tori's right supporting leg is at a 45–90 degree angle to the uke. Depending on the situation, tori may push uke with his right hand.

Combination hidari ko-soto-gari – hidari de-ashi-harai

▶ Tori has a right-handed grip and uke a left-handed grip. Uke counters tori's hidari ko-soto-gari by stepping backwards with his left foot. Tori pushes uke with his left hand so that uke is forced to step backwards with his right foot. Tori sweeps uke's left foot diagonally to the front.

De-ashi-harai with one hand as uke retreats

▶ In the initial position, tori and uke have a one-handed grip. Tori blocks uke's left hand grip by grabbing uke's left wrist. Tori pushes uke by the wrist. When uke retreats with his left foot, tori sweeps uke's right foot diagonally to the front.

De-ashi-harai in jigotai position as uke pulls back

▶ Uke moves backwards and pulls tori strongly towards himself or sideways. Tori sweeps uke's right foot as it comes off the mat.

DE-ASHI-HARAI EXERCISES

▶ Tandoku-renshu or solo practice is essential, especially for de-ashi-harai, to achieve the correct rhythm, timing and speed. The foot sweeps de-ashi-harai, okuri-ashi-harai and harai-tsurikomi-ashi are performed from uke's movement. Ashi-waza specialists perform several hundred repetitions daily. Solo practice can be enhanced by the use of assistive devices such as hand and leg weights and resistance bands. See page 32.

COMBINATIONS FOLLOWING DE-ASHI-HARAI
(can be combined with almost all throws)

- ▶ seoi-nage
- ▶ migi or hidari ippon-seoi-nage
- ▶ o-goshi
- ▶ hiza-guruma
- ▶ o-soto-gari, page 80
- ▶ de-ashi-harai
- ▶ okuri-ashi-harai
- ▶ ko-soto-gari
- ▶ ko-soto-gake
- ▶ tai-otoshi, page 100, 101
- ▶ hidari uchi-mata, page 126
- ▶ harai-goshi, page 136
- ▶ koshi-guruma, page 94
- ▶ tsurikomi-goshi, page 88
- ▶ hidari sode-tsurikomi-goshi
- ▶ tani-otoshi
- ▶ ura-nage
- ▶ kesa-gatame/yoko-shiho-gatame, page 153
- ▶ juji-gatame, page 166

COUNTER-THROWS, KAESHI-WAZAS TO DE-ASHI-HARAI

- ▶ ko-uchi-gari, page 64
- ▶ o-uchi-gari, page 71
- ▶ o-soto-gari ken-ken
- ▶ ko-soto-gari ken-ken
- ▶ tsubame-gaeshi, page 53
- ▶ morote-seoi-nage, ippon-seoi-nage
- ▶ tai-otoshi

TSUBAME-GAESHI – SWALLOW SWOOP – COUNTER THROW

- ▶ Uke sweeps tori's right foot with de-ashi-harai or okuri-ashi-harai. Tori dodges the throw attempt by bending his knee. Tori continues the move by sweeping uke's left leg with the same foot diagonally to the front. Depending on the situation, tori may do a ko-soto-gake on uke's left foot.

USE OF HANDS IN ASHI-WAZA AND DIRECTION OF FOOT SWEEP

▶ The foot sweeps, that is, ashi-wazas: de-ashi-harai, okuri-ashi-harai and harai-tsurikomi-ashi, plus sasae-tsurikomi-ashi and hiza-guruma, form a set of throws that support each other for the competitor and should therefore all be practised. The differences in the foot sweeps are in the way of using hands and the sweeping direction of uke's foot.

Harai-tsurikomi-ashi

Use of hands: tsukuri, hands push and kuzushi, hands lift-pull.
Foot sweep: backwards in the direction of uke's right foot.

Okuri-ashi-harai

Use of hands: tsukuri, left hand pushing to the side and right hand lifting slightly. Finally, strong downward pull of both hands.
Foot sweep: to the side and feet together.

De-ashi-harai

Use of hands: tsukuri, hands guiding uke's movement. Finally, the left hand pulls down strongly with the right hand helping.
Foot sweep: forward.

OKURI-ASHI-HARAI – DOUBLE FOOT SWEEP

▶ In okuri-ashi-harai, tori and uke facing each other move sideways. Tori sweeps at the ankle of uke's right foot towards uke's left foot. In a variation, tori may sweep with tori's thigh against uke's thigh. If necessary, tori gives the movement additional momentum by pushing with his left hand and slightly raising his right hand. The throw ends with a strong downward pull of both hands. Okuri-ashi-harai requires good timing.

Combinations:
▶ migi grip hidari ko-soto-gari – hidari de-ashi-harai – hidari okuri-ashi-harai/hidari ko-soto-gake
▶ ko-uchi-gari – okuri-ashi-harai
▶ hidari hiza-guruma – migi okuri-ashi-harai

HARAI-TSURIKOMI-ASHI – LIFT-PULL FOOT SWEEP

   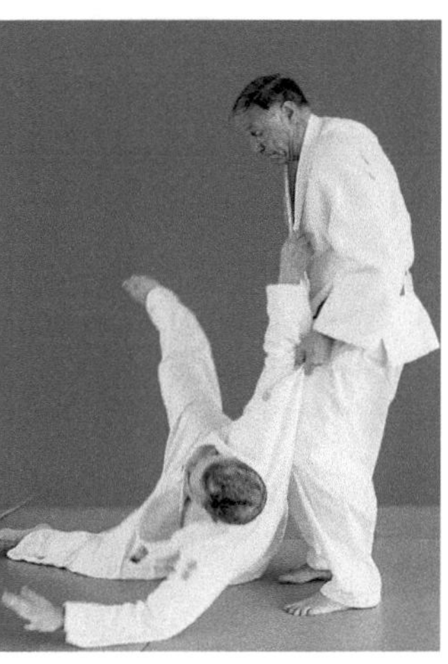

▶ Uke steps back with his right foot. Tori follows and steps his right foot close to uke's left foot. Tori pushes, lifts and pulls uke strongly with his hands and simultaneously sweeps uke's right leg backwards past uke's left leg. Finally, tori turns uke in the air with his hands, causing uke to land in front of tori.

Combination feint hidari o-soto-gari – harai-tsurikomi-ashi

▶ Tori performs a feint of hidari o-soto-gari or repeated feints. Tori acts as if about to start an o-soto-gari, but does a harai-tsurikomi-ashi by pushing uke and stepping first with his right foot in front of uke's left foot.

SASAE-TSURIKOMI-ASHI – SUPPORTING FOOT LIFT-PULL THROW

▶ Tori stops the advancing uke's right foot by placing the sole of his left foot at uke's right ankle. Tori lifts and pulls uke strongly towards himself, after which tori rotates his body to the left. Uke is thrown over the ankle support point to the mat.

Combination hidari tai-otoshi – sasae-tsurikomi-ashi

▶ Uke has countered tai-otoshi by stepping over tori's left leg. Tori reverses the pull to the migi side and steps his right foot in front of uke's left foot and finishes with a sasae-tsurikomi-ashi.

Sasae-tsurikomi-ashi with different grips

▶ Tori takes a grip on uke's right armpit with his left hand, his arm being above uke's right arm. Tori can throw uke to either side.
▶ Tori takes a grip with both hands on uke's armpits. His arms are under uke's arms. The kake phase of the throw requires tori to have a very strong body rotation.

COMBINATIONS FOLLOWING SASAE-TSURIKOMI-ASHI

▶ de-ashi-harai, page 48
▶ hiza-guruma, page 57
▶ sasae-tsurikomi-ashi
▶ o-uchi-gari
▶ ko-uchi-gari
▶ o-soto-gari
▶ morote-seoi-nage, page 112

HIZA-GURUMA – KNEE WHEEL

▶ Tori breaks uke's balance by pulling hard diagonally to the front. Tori places the sole of his left foot to the side or front of uke's knee and prevents uke from moving forward. Tori throws uke over his outstretched leg ("wheel axle") using the force of his upper body, by turning his body.

The combination of hidari sasae-tsurikomi-ashi – hiza-guruma

▶ Uke counters hidari sasae-tsurikomi-ashi by stepping over tori's foot. Tori reverses the throw to the opposite side and makes a migi hiza-guruma.

KO-UCHI-GARI · KO-UCHI-MAKIKOMI · KO-UCHI-GAESHI

O-UCHI-GARI · O-UCHI-GAESHI

KO-SOTO-GARI · KO-SOTO-GAKE

KO-UCHI-GARI – SMALL INNER REAP

▶ Tori enters with tsugi-ashi his right foot ahead. Breaking uke's balance (kuzushi), is done at the same time as the first step. The left hand pulls downward and the right forearm makes contact with uke's upper body. Tori sweeps uke's right leg with his right foot, with his leg straight, with the foot bent inwards, the hips in front and the supporting leg bent. Tori pushes with his right hand backwards to the right. In the throwing phase (kake), tori's body follows and often ends up on top of uke, allowing tori to continue with mat techniques.

KO-UCHI-GARI GRIPS (KUMIKATA)

Tori's right hand pushes uke under his chin.	Tori's right hand is on uke's back in jigotai.	Tori's right hand is on uke's back under his sleeve.	Both hands are on uke's lapels.	Both hands are on uke's right armpit.

PREPARATORY ACTIONS (TSUKURI) FOR KO-UCHI-GARI

Jerk forward – push.

Pressing down – push.

Pull to the right side.   Lifting – pressing down – pushing.

VARIATIONS AND SITUATIONS FOR APPLYING KO-UCHI-GARI

   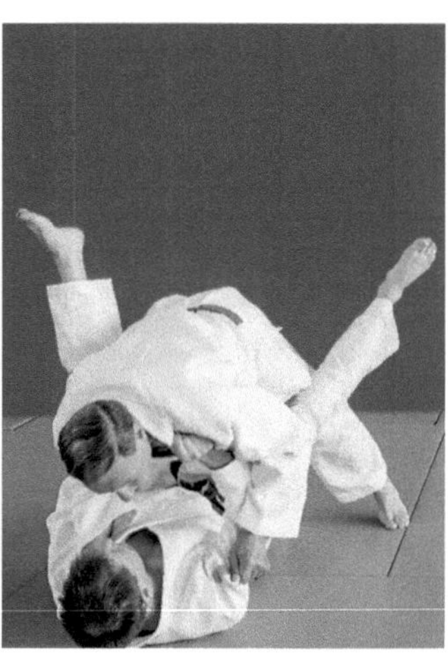

Ko-uchi-gari, uke steps forward with his right foot

▶ Uke steps forward with his right foot. Tori retreats with his left foot with tai-sabaki and sweeps
   uke's right foot before the full weight of uke's body has shifted to the foot. If tori sweeps uke's
   right foot before it properly touches the mat, the throw is often called a ko-uchi-harai.

Ko-uchi-gari, uke steps with his right foot to the side

▶ Tori follows uke's move to the right with his left foot step. Tori sweeps uke's right foot
   with the right foot before the full weight of uke's body has shifted to the foot.

Ko-uchi-gari jumping (ken-ken)

▶ Tori has a normal grip and he presses uke down with his hands or his left hand is over uke's right hand in uke's right lapel or under uke's arm in his armpit and simultaneously moves forward with tsugi-ashi with his left foot close to uke. Tori traps uke's right foot with the foot of his right leg and prevents uke from moving backwards. Tori pushes uke and jumps forward on his left supporting leg until uke is thrown onto his back.

Ko-uchi-gari with tori's two steps

▶ Tori steps with his left foot in front of uke's right foot at the same time he makes a kuzushi. Tori's right foot immediately follows and sweeps uke's right foot.

Ko-uchi-gari from the defensive position, jigotai

▶ Tori jerks defensive uke, momentarily relaxes the pressure on uke and simultaneously sweeps uke's right foot with his right foot.

Ko-uchi-gari with a one-handed grip

▶ Tori and uke have a one-handed grip in the starting position. Tori uses his right tsurite hand to pull uke towards him and simultaneously steps with his left foot to the left. Before the weight of uke's body has shifted to uke's right foot, tori sweeps uke's foot. At the end, tori grabs uke's right hand and guides the throw to the end.

Combination feint uchi-mata – ko-uchi-gari (1)

▶ Tori jumps on his left foot close to uke's left foot as if to make an uchi-mata. Uke counters by stepping backwards with his left foot. Tori uses his right foot to sweep uke's right foot.

Combination uchi-mata – ko-uchi-gari (2)

▶ Uke blocks tori's uchi-mata in the sweep phase. Tori reverses the throw and sweeps uke's right foot with his right foot.

Combination o-uchi-gari – ko-uchi-gari

▶ Uke blocks tori's o-uchi-gari. Tori changes the direction of the right foot sweep and sweeps uke's right foot.

Combination of morote, ippon and eri-seoi-nage – ko-uchi-gari

▶ Tori enters ippon-seoi-nage with his right foot first. Uke counters the throw by straightening his body. Tori reverses the direction of the throw and catches uke's right foot with his right foot.

Combination tai-otoshi – ko-uchi-gari

▶ Uke counters tai-otoshi by stepping over tori's outstretched leg. Tori continues with ko-uchi-gari.

Ko-uchi-gari kaeshi-waza to uke's de-ashi-harai

▶ Uke's timing in the sweep phase of the de-ashi-harai fails. Tori shifts his body
weight to his left foot and sweeps uke's right foot with his right foot.

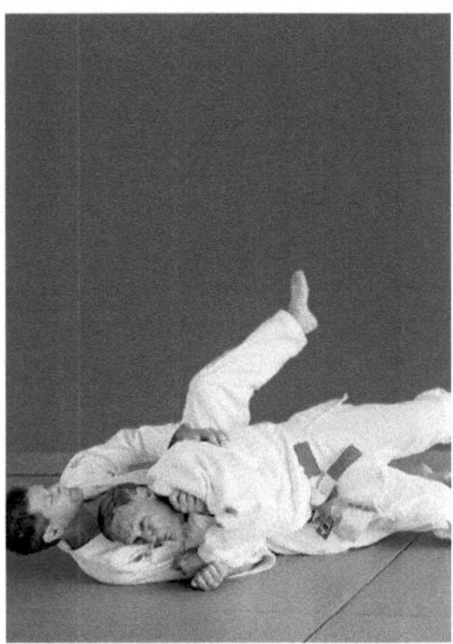

A variation of ko-uchi-gari, KO-UCHI-MAKIKOMI (yoko-sutemi-waza) – minor inner winding throw

▶ Tori pulls uke as if doing ippon-seoi-nage. Tori takes advantage of uke's counter reaction and goes deep between
uke's legs with tsugi-ashi, hooking uke's right leg with his right foot. Tori throws himself forward, attached
to uke. If the competition rules do not allow leg gripping, tori keeps his right arm wrapped around uke's
right arm during the throw. The throw is also made with both hands on uke's right lower sleeve.

A variation of ko-uchi-gari, ko-uchi-harai – a small inside sweep

▶ As uke moves forward or to the side with his right foot, tori will sweep uke's right foot with ko-uchi-gari before the
weight of uke's body is transferred to this foot. Depending on the situation, the hand action is the same as in de-ashi-
harai, i.e. both hands pull straight down, or as in gari throws, the left hand pulls forward and the right hand pushes.

Ko-uchi-gari variation, between tori's legs

▶ Tori steps with his left foot in front of uke's right foot. Tori sweeps (ko-uchi-gari)/
hooks (ko-uchi-gake) with his right leg uke's right foot between tori's legs.

   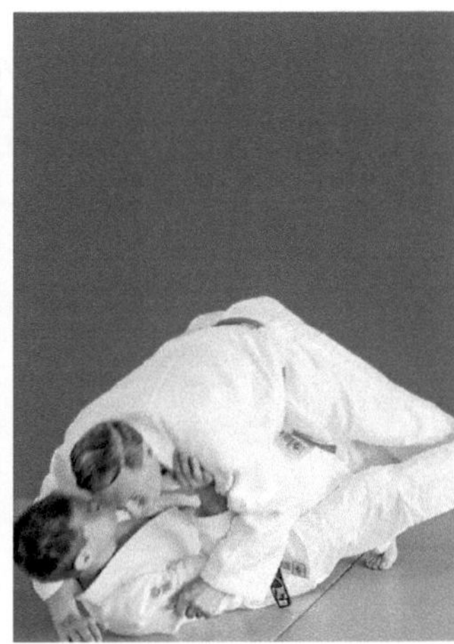

Variation of ko-uchi-gari, ko-uchi-gake – small inner hook

▶ Tori does ko-uchi-gari by hooking his right leg on the calf of the uke's right leg, as in ko-soto-gake.

KO-UCHI-GARI EXERCISES

Single-leg jumps
forward and backward

Pressing against uke

Uchi-komi without a grip while stationary
as well as in motion

Tandoku-renshu with
resistance bands

COMBINATIONS FOLLOWING KO-UCHI-GARI

- ▶ o-uchi-gari, page 70
- ▶ o-soto-gari
- ▶ uchi-mata
- ▶ tai-otoshi, page 100
- ▶ migi or hidari ippon-seoi-nage, page 119
- ▶ tomoe-nage, page 143

COUNTER-THROWS, KAESHI-WAZAS TO KO-UCHI-GARI

- ▶ de-ashi-harai
- ▶ hiza-guruma
- ▶ o-soto-gari
- ▶ ippon-seoi-nage
- ▶ tsurikomi-goshi
- ▶ tomoe-nage, page 143
- ▶ uki-waza
- ▶ ko-uchi-gaeshi, page 66

KO-UCHI-GAESHI (te-waza) – small inner reaping throw counter

- ▶ Tori dodges uke's ko-uchi-gari with a right foot lift. Tori takes advantage of uke's poor balance and throws uke with his hands either to the right or to the left.

O-UCHI-GARI – LARGE INNER REAP

▶ Tori enters with tsugi-ashi with his right foot in front. Breaking the balance (kuzushi), is done at the same time as the entry step. Tori's left hand pulls diagonally down and his right forearm makes contact with uke's upper body. Tori sweeps with the calf of his right leg in a wide semicircular arc the calf of uke's left leg. Tori pushes uke to the right backwards. In the throwing phase (kake), tori's body follows uke and often ends up on top of uke, giving tori a good opportunity to continue on the mat.

O-UCHI-GARI GRIPS (KUMIKATA)

Tori's right hand is on uke's back in jigotai

Tori's right hand is on uke's back under his armpit

Both hands are on uke's lapels

PREPARATORY ACTIONS (TSUKURI) FOR O-UCHI-GARI

Pull forward – push

Push down – push

Pull to the left – and then to the right   Lifting – pressing down – pushing

VARIATIONS AND SITUATIONS FOR APPLYING O-UCHI-GARI

O-uchi-gari, uke steps forward with his left foot
▶ Uke steps forward with his left foot. Tori moves his left foot in front of uke's right foot
  and pulls uke towards him. Tori sweeps uke's left leg with his right leg.

O-uchi-gari, uke moves in a circular motion with his left foot
▶ Uke steps to the side with his left foot in a circular motion. Tori uses his right hand
  to pull uke towards him and uses his right leg to sweep uke's left leg.

O-uchi-gari jumping (ken-ken)

▶ Tori has a basic grip or his left hand under uke's armpit and he lifts uke upwards and simultaneously moves forward with tsugi-ashi close to uke. Tori presses uke downwards with his hands, catches uke's left leg with his right leg. Tori pushes uke with his hands and hops forward on the supporting leg until uke is thrown onto his back.

O-uchi-gari on two steps of tori

▶ Uke has a left grip (kenka-yotsu). Tori steps forward with his left foot between uke's legs and simultaneously makes a kuzushi. Tori's right leg immediately follows and sweeps uke's left leg.

O-uchi-gari with one-handed grip

▶ Tori and uke have a one-handed grip, for example in the starting situation. Tori pulls uke strongly with his right hand and his body so that uke is forced to step forward with his left foot. Tori uses his right leg to sweep uke's left leg. At the end of the throw, tori also catches uke with his left hand and guides him to finish the throw.

Combination uchi-mata – o-uchi-gari

▶ Uke counters uchi-mata in the sweep phase by straightening his body. Tori reverses the direction of the throw and sweeps uke's left leg with his right leg.

Combination ko-uchi-gari – o-uchi-gari

▶ Uke counters tori's ko-uchi-gari by moving his right foot backwards. Tori changes the direction of the right leg sweep and sweeps uke's left leg.

Combination feint o-soto-gari – o-uchi-gari

▶ Tori does a feint of o-soto-gari or repeated feints (tsukuri) in front of uke by stepping with his left foot close to uke's right foot as if he is going to do a ken-ken o-soto-gari. Uke counters by stepping backwards with his right foot, causing tori to change the direction of the movement of his right foot and sweeps uke's left leg.

Combination morote-seoi-nage – o-uchi-gari

▶ Uke counters tori's feint morote-seoi-nage or ippon-seoi-nage. Tori reverses the direction of the throw and sweeps uke's left leg with his right leg.

O-uchi-gari kaeshi-waza to uke's de-ashi-harai

▶ Uke's timing in de-ashi-harai fails. Tori moves his right foot between uke's legs and sweeps uke's left leg with his right leg.

O-uchi-gari kaeshi-waza to uke's hidari sasae-tsurikomi-ashi/hiza-guruma

▶ Uke makes a hidari sasae-tsurikomi-ashi or hidari hiza-guruma with his right foot on tori's left foot. Tori anticipates the throw attempt and sweeps uke's left leg with his right leg.

Variation of o-uchi-gari, o-uchi-harai – large inner sweep

▶ Tori steps forward or to the side with his left foot. Tori sweeps uke's left leg with his right leg with o-uchi-gari before the weight of uke's body is transferred to the foot. Depending on the situation, the hand action is the same as in harai, where both hands pull straight down, or as in gari, where the left hand pulls forward and the right hand pushes.

O-UCHI-GARI EXERCISES

Single-leg jumps forward and backward

Push against uke

Uchi-komi without grip on the spot and from movement

Tandoku-renshu with resistance bands

COMBINATIONS FOLLOWING O-UCHI-GARI

▶ ko-uchi-gari, page 63
▶ o-soto-gari, page 80
▶ tsurikomi-goshi, page 89
▶ uchi-mata, page 128
▶ tai-otoshi, page 100
▶ morote-seoi-nage, page 111
▶ for hidari and migi ippon-seoi-nage, page 120
▶ tomoe-nage, page 143
▶ hiza-guruma
▶ okuri-ashi-harai
▶ de-ashi-harai
▶ kesa-gatame, page 153

COUNTER-THROWS, KAESHI-WAZAS TO O-UCHI-GARI

- ▶ de-ashi-harai, page 49
- ▶ ko-soto-gake
- ▶ uchi-mata, page 132
- ▶ tai-otoshi
- ▶ seoi-nage
- ▶ tomoe-nage
- ▶ ura-nage
- ▶ o-uchi-gaeshi, page 73

O-UCHI-GAESHI (te-waza) – large inner reaping throw counter

- ▶ Tori dodges uke's o-uchi-gari with a left leg lift. Tori takes advantage of uke's poor balance and throws uke with his hands, turning either to the right or to the left.

KO-SOTO-GARI – SMALL OUTER REAP

- ▶ Uke is stationary or advancing with his right foot. Tori steps with tsugi-ashi left foot in front next to uke's right foot. The right foot follows behind and steps behind his left foot. Tori's left hand pulls down and right forearm makes contact with uke's chest. Tori sweeps with the sole of his left foot uke's right heel in the direction of uke's toes. Simultaneously with the sweep, tori straightens his right arm and pushes uke to the mat. In the two-step variation, tori first steps with the right foot next to uke's right foot. The left foot follows and sweeps uke's right foot.

COMBINATIONS FOLLOWING KO-SOTO-GARI

- ▶ hidari or migi de-ashi-harai, page 51
- ▶ o-uchi-gari
- ▶ morote-seoi-nage, page 111
- ▶ harai-goshi, page 136

VARIATIONS AND SITUATIONS FOR APPLYING KO-SOTO-GARI

Ko-soto-gari straight backwards

▶ Tori places his left foot behind uke's right ankle and jumps with his right foot next to uke. Tori pulls uke towards himself, sweeps uke's right foot with his left foot and with powerful push with his hands, pushes uke onto his back.

▶ In the yoko-gake version, tori throws himself on the mat with uke.

Combination o-soto-gari – nidan-ko-soto-gari

▶ Uke counters tori's o-soto-gari by moving his left foot back. Tori puts his right foot down on the mat, turns uke to the left with his hands and sweeps uke's left foot with his left foot.

Ko-soto-gari kaeshi-waza – to tai-otoshi

▶ Tori counters uke's tai-otoshi by stepping his right foot to the side of uke's outstretched leg and continues the move by doing ko-soto-gari.

Ko-soto-gari – kaeshi-waza from behind

▶ Uke attacks with a forward throw as with harai-goshi. Tori counters the throw by lowering his centre of gravity and pulling uke tightly into contact with himself. Tori sweeps with his left foot a nidan-ko-soto-gari at uke's supporting leg.

KO-SOTO-GAKE – SMALL OUTER HOOK

▶ Tori steps forward next to uke's right foot with tsugi-ashi (left-right foot). Tori's left foot hooks with the sole or calf of his left leg to the outside of uke's right ankle or from behind at his calf. In the leg hook phase, tori lifts uke up with both hands and finally pushes uke towards the mat.

VARIATIONS AND SITUATIONS FOR APPLYING KO-SOTO-GAKE

Ko-soto-gake variation with two steps

▶ Tori enters the ko-soto-gake by stepping his right foot next to uke's right foot. Tori hooks uke's right leg with his left foot.

O-SOTO-GARI · O-SOTO-GAESHI · O-SOTO-OTOSHI
O-SOTO-GURUMA · O-SOTO-MAKIKOMI

O-SOTO-GARI – LARGE OUTER REAP

▶ Tori pulls uke sideways downwards with his left hand so that uke's balance is shifted to his right foot. At the same time, tori uses his right hand to make contact with uke's left chest. Tori steps with his left foot next to uke in line with uke's feet and makes right chest contact with uke's right chest. With a quick swing of his right leg, tori catches uke's leg at the kneecap and pushes uke towards the mat with his right hand.

O-SOTO-GARI GRIPS

Tori's right hand is on the back of uke's neck

Yama-arashi -grip

Soto-makikomi -grip

Tori has both hands are on uke's lapels

Tori's right hand knuckles are on uke's chin

Tori's right wrist is elbow up on uke's chin

PREPARATORY ACTIONS (TSUKURI) FOR O-SOTO-GARI

Pull forward – push   Pressing down – pushing   Pull to the right – to the left

VARIATIONS AND SITUATIONS FOR APPLYING O-SOTO-GARI

O-soto-gari variation, sweep with the thigh

▶ Tori uses his left hand to pull uke horizontally to the side and right hand to push uke up to the rear left. Tori's knuckles or wrist are at the side of uke's neck. Tori makes upper body contact with uke. Tori reaps with the back of his right leg against the back of uke's right leg. Tori pulls uke down with his left hand and pushes uke towards the mat with his right hand. This variation also works in a kenka-yotsu situation.

O-soto-gari variation, jumping (ken-ken)

▶ From a distance, tori slides his right foot to the side of uke's knee and uses his hands to twist uke's body to the left in a tilted position, pushing hard with his hands and feet so that uke's right leg bends at the knee. Tori jumps or hops with his left foot to uke's side, then reaps uke straight on his back with one or more jumps. This variation also works in a kenka-yotsu situation.

O-soto-gari when uke is standing up

▶ Uke stands up from a kneeling position with right foot in front. Tori takes advantage of uke's poor balance and easily performs an o-soto-gari. Tori has the opportunity to continue on the mat, for example by taking a kesa-gatame.

O-soto-gari with uke stepping backwards

▶ Uke steps backwards with his right foot. Tori pushes and presses down with his left hand on uke's right hand and his right hand controls uke's head. Tori takes a quick, long step with his left foot to uke's side and finishes the o-soto-gari.

O-soto-gari with a one-handed grip

▶ Tori and uke have a one-handed grip in the initial position. Tori unexpectedly pulls uke strongly with his left hand diagonally to the front and at the same time steps into the o-soto-gari with his left foot. Tori tosses his right hand to the right or left side of uke's head and immediately reaps uke's right leg with his right leg.

Combination feint hidari de-ashi-harai – migi o-soto-gari

▶ Tori uses his right foot to make a de-ashi-harai feint sweep to uke's left foot, which uke dodges by moving his left foot back. Tori enters migi o-soto-gari and throws uke.

Combination ko-soto-gari or ko-soto-gake – o-soto-gari

▶ Tori makes a ko-soto-gari or ko-soto-gake, which uke counters by stepping back with his right foot. Tori takes a long step with his left foot close to uke's right foot and makes an o-soto-gari.

Combination hidari ko-soto-gari – migi o-uchi-gari – o-soto-gari

▶ Uke counters a hidari ko-soto-gari and then a migi o-uchi-gari by stepping back with his left foot. Tori enters migi o-soto-gari with his left foot and reaps uke's right leg.

Combination uchi-mata – o-soto-gari

▶ Uke dodges tori's uchi-mata. Tori turns his body to the left, enters the o-soto-gari with his left foot and reaps uke's right leg with his right leg.

Combination hidari hiza-guruma/hidari sasae-tsurikomi-ashi – migi o-soto-gari

▶ Tori unbalances uke as if to make hidari sasae-tsurikomi-ashi. Tori's weight is on his right foot. In the middle of the pull, tori switches his weight to his left foot with a small jump forward, while switching the pull of his right hand to a push. His left hand pulls down and his right leg very quickly reaps uke's right leg.

Combination koshi-guruma/sode-tsurikomi-goshi – o-soto-gari or o-soto-otoshi

▶ Uke counters tori's koshi-guruma or sode-tsurikomi-goshi. Tori moves his right leg behind uke's right leg and reaps uke's right leg or makes o-soto-otoshi or, if necessary, a jumping o-soto-gari (ken-ken).

Combination of ippon, morote or eri-seoi-nage – o-soto-gari or o-soto-otoshi

▶ Uke counters tori's seoi-nage. Tori reverses the direction of the throw and places his right foot on uke's right knee bend. Depending on the situation, tori makes a jumping reap (ken-ken) or makes an o-soto-otoshi.

O-SOTO-GARI EXERCISES

Jumping back and forth on one foot

Jumps in pairs with a chase

Pressing against a rigid uke

Three person uchi-komi (power uchi-komi)

COMBINATIONS FOLLOWING O-SOTO-GARI

▶ de-ashi-harai, page 49
▶ sasae-tsurikomi-ashi
▶ harai-tsurikomi-ashi, page 56
▶ ko-soto-gari, page 74
▶ o-uchi-gari
▶ morote-seoi-otoshi, page 111
▶ hidari ippon-seoi-nage, page 120
▶ tai-otoshi, page 101
▶ harai-goshi
▶ uchi-mata, page 131
▶ ashi-guruma, page 138
▶ koshi-guruma, page 94
▶ yoko-tomoe-nage, page 142
▶ tani-otoshi, page 147

COUNTER-THROWS, KAESHI-WAZAS TO O-SOTO-GARI

▶ ko-soto-gake
▶ uki-otoshi (te-waza)
▶ tani-otoshi
▶ tai-otoshi
▶ ura-nage, page 146
▶ morote-seoi-nage, page 112
▶ utsuri-goshi
▶ ushiro-goshi
▶ harai-goshi
▶ o-soto-otoshi
▶ o-soto-gaeshi, page 83

O-SOTO-GAESHI – large outer reaping throw counter

▶ Uke tries to throw tori with o-soto-gari. Tori stops uke's throw by stepping back with his left foot. Tori pushes uke with his upper body and reaps uke's right leg with his right foot.

O-SOTO-OTOSHI – major outer drop

▶ Tori enters an o-soto-gari. Tori stomps his right foot down to the rear, drops his body and pushes uke to the mat.

O-SOTO-GURUMA – large outer wheel

▶ Tori enters o-soto-gari next to uke. Tori reaps both of uke's legs with his outstretched right leg.

O-SOTO-MAKIKOMI (yoko-sutemi-waza) – large outside wraparound throw to the mat

▶ After the o-soto-gari attempt, tori moves his right hand over uke's head and wraps uke's arm around his own. Tori throws himself onto the mat, with uke following.

TSURIKOMI-GOSHI · SODE-TSURIKOMI-GOSHI

O-GOSHI · TSURI-GOSHI · KOSHI-GURUMA

USHIRO-GOSHI · UTSURI-GOSHI

TSURIKOMI-GOSHI – LIFT-PULL HIP THROW

- Tsurikomi goshi is an important basic throw for hip, upper arm and some hand throws because of the way it is done. It is a good idea to include a practice of tsurikomi-goshi at the beginning of your training.

- Tori breaks uke's balance to the front or diagonally to the front. Tori steps his right foot forward between uke's feet (step 1), moves his left foot forward (step 2) pivoting on the ball of his right foot and then moves his right foot (step 3) forward in front of uke's right foot. During the first step, tori pushes his right elbow into uke's left armpit and makes firm side and hip contact with uke. Tori throws uke by descending with his back straight below uke's centre of gravity and then straightening his legs. Tori finishes the throw by leaning forward and twisting his body to the left. Tori continues to push and pull the arms to the end.

TSURIKOMI-GOSHI GRIPS (KUMIKATA)

Tori's right hand is on uke's back and the left hand is on the right cuff

Tori's left hand is on uke's right lapel

Tori's right and left hands are on uke's left lapel

PREPARATORY ACTIONS (TSUKURI) FOR TSURIKOMI-GOSHI

Tori first presses uke down and then lifts it up

Tori pushes and when uke reacts against it, tori pulls

VARIATIONS AND SITUATIONS FOR APPLYING TSURIKOMI-GOSHI

Tsurikomi-goshi with tori taking two steps forward

▶ Tori steps right foot in front of uke's right foot and left foot with 90 degree tai-sabaki in front of uke's left foot. Tori finishes the throw.

Tsurikomi-goshi as uke advances

▶ Uke steps forward with his right foot. Tori pulls and lifts uke forward and drops himself right foot first in front of uke's feet. Tori straightens his legs, leans forward and throws uke with speed.

Tsurikomi-goshi, with tori's right hand gripping uke's back

▶ Uke has a defensive stance and a left hand grip. Tori takes hold of uke's back with his right hand. Tori breaks uke's balance in the direction of uke's toes. Tori takes a long step with his right foot under uke and finishes the throw.

Tsurikomi-goshi – Tori has both hands on uke's left lapel

▶ Uke has a left side grip. Uke prevents tori from getting a left hand grip. Tori's right hand grip is on uke's left collar. Tori has a left hand grip on uke's left lapel under his right arm. Tori enters the tsurikomi-goshi and finishes the throw.

Combination feint hidari de-ashi-harai – tsurikomi-goshi

▶ Tori uses his right foot to perform a feint of hidari de-ashi-harai to uke's left leg. Tori swings his right leg without lowering it in front of uke's right foot and the left foot in front of uke's left foot. Tori finishes with a tsurikomi-goshi.

Combination o-uchi-gari – tsurikomi-goshi

▶ Uke counters tori's o-uchi-gari by lifting his left leg up. Tori pivots on his right
foot into the throw. Tori finishes with a tsurikomi-goshi.

Combination ko-uchi-gari – tsurikomi-goshi

▶ Uke counters tori's ko-uchi-gari by stepping back with his right foot. Tori follows uke
with a long right foot step in front of uke's right foot. The left foot follows tori's entry.
Tori finishes the tsurikomi-goshi and throws uke diagonally to the front.

TSURIKOMI-GOSHI EXERCISES

Squats with uke on the back   Three person uchi-komi (power uchi-komi)

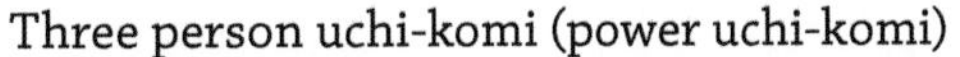

COMBINATIONS FOLLOWING TSURIKOMI-GOSHI

- ▶ o-uchi-gari
- ▶ ko-uchi-gari
- ▶ o-soto-gari
- ▶ uchi-mata
- ▶ harai-goshi
- ▶ tai-otoshi
- ▶ soto-makikomi
- ▶ tomoe-nage

COUNTER-THROWS (KAESHI-WAZA) TO TSURIKOMI-GOSHI

- ▶ ko-soto-gake
- ▶ utsuri-goshi
- ▶ ushiro-goshi
- ▶ tomoe-nage
- ▶ ura-nage
- ▶ uki-waza

SODE-TSURIKOMI-GOSHI – sleeve lift-pull hip throw

▶ Tori grabs uke's right sleeve with his left hand and the left cuff with his right hand, in a variation the hand turns from the cuff or from the left elbow. Tori breaks uke's balance (kuzushi) by pulling forward. Tori steps with his right foot in front of uke's right foot and with his left foot in front of uke's left foot with a 90-degree tai-sabaki. Tori pulls uke onto his back and crouches down. Tori raises and pushes uke's left arm and continues to pull forward with his left arm. Tori straightens his legs, twists his body to the left and throws uke over his hips and side.

VARIATIONS AND SITUATIONS FOR APPLYING SODE-TSURIKOMI-GOSHI

Sode-tsurikomi-goshi turning (mawari)

▶ Tori breaks uke's balance (kuzushi) to the left as if making a throw to the left. Tori steps with his left
foot in front of uke's left foot, changes the direction of the hands to the right and
pivots on his left foot to the right. Tori finishes the sode-tsurikomi-goshi forward.

Sode-tsurikomi-goshi, sweep with tori's right foot

▶ Uke counters tori's sode-tsurikomi-goshi by moving his right foot past tori's hip.
Tori lifts his right leg off the mat and uses it to sweep uke's right leg.

Sode-tsurikomi-goshi, with both hands on uke's left sleeve

▶ Tori takes hold of the cuff of uke's left sleeve with his right hand and the inside of the same cuff with his left
hand. Tori pulls uke strongly towards himself, entering first with his right foot and then with his left. Tori
pulls uke's left hand firmly to his chest. Tori finishes the throw by twisting his body strongly to the left.

Sode-tsurikomi-goshi, tori's grip is on uke's left sleeve and left lapel

▶ Uke and Tori have a right-handed stance. Tori's right hand grip is from the cuff or elbow of uke's left hand. Uke prevents tori from taking a left hand grip. Tori grabs uke's left lapel with his left hand. Tori enters the throw, pulling uke onto his back. Tori finishes the sode-tsurikomi-goshi with a strong left twist.

Sode-tsurikomi-goshi-otoshi – sleeve lift-pull hip throw dropping on one knee or throwing on both knees

▶ Tori moves uke strongly forward with his arms and body. Tori enters the throw by stepping forward with his right foot. The left foot follows next to the right foot, after which tori drops onto his right knee or drops onto both knees in front of uke. Tori's right foot comes in between uke's legs or outside the right leg. Tori finishes the throw.

O-GOSHI – LARGE HIP THROW

▶ Tori breaks uke's balance (kuzushi) forward. Tori enters with his right foot in front of uke's right foot. At the same time as tori moves his left foot in front of uke's left foot, tori moves his right hand under uke's left arm on uke's back close to uke's belt. Tori pulls uke into a tight contact with his hip and side. Tori first bends his knees, then straightens his legs and throws uke over his hips.

O-goshi, tori and uke in opposite stances

▶ Tori has his right hand on uke's back under his armpit. Tori breaks uke's balance (kuzushi) in the direction shown by his toes. Tori takes a long step with his right foot in front of uke's right foot and his left foot follows in front of uke's left foot. Tori finishes the o-goshi. O-goshi is also performed in a grip fight situation. Tori blocks uke's left hand grip with his right hand and moves it to uke's back.

TSURI-GOSHI – LIFTING HIP THROW

Tori grabs uke's belt from under his left arm (ko-tsuri-goshi, small lifting hip)

Tori takes hold of uke's belt over the shoulder (o-tsuri-goshi, large lifting hip)

KOSHI-GURUMA – HIP WHEEL

▶ Tori wraps his right arm firmly around uke's neck. Tori pushes his hip past uke's right side. During the throwing phase, tori's hip and upper body act as a kind of axle for a wheel.

Koshi-guruma – the right foot is deep in between uke's legs
- ▶ Tori has a migi shizentai stance. Tori's left hand is on uke's right collar and the right hand takes a grip around uke's neck. Tori steps his left foot next to his right foot with the toes pointing towards uke's right foot. Immediately tori moves his right foot deep in between uke's legs. In the throwing phase (kake), tori can swing his right leg up off the ground. Tori follows uke onto the mat.

Combination hidari de-ashi-harai or feint de-ashi-harai – koshi-guruma
- ▶ Tori sweeps uke's left foot and moves it directly in front of uke's right foot.

Combination o-soto-gari – koshi-guruma
- ▶ Tori presses with his right foot on Uke's right foot as if doing a ken-ken o-soto-gari (jumping). Uke pushes back with his body. Tori drops his right foot down and moves his right hand to uke's neck. Tori reverses the throw forward and finishes the koshi-guruma by rolling to the mat.

COMBINATION FROM KOSHI-GURUMA
- ▶ O-soto-gari or o-soto-otoshi, page 81

WAYS OF FINISHING KOSHI-GURUMA

▶ Right knee on the ground between uke's legs

▶ Swinging the right leg and throwing oneself to the mat

USHIRO-GOSHI – REAR HIP

▶ Tori counters uke's hip throw by bending his legs, holding his hips in front and dropping below uke's hips. Tori grabs his left hand around uke's waist. Tori straightens his legs and lifts uke high in the air and drops down onto his back. In the drop phase, tori may step back to gain more room for the throw (Pictures 1–3.) In the counter-throw to ko-uchi-gari, o-uchi-gari, o-soto-gari, etc., tori may use his left leg to lift uke up before the drop phase of the throw (Picture 4).

UTSURI-GOSHI – CHANGING HIP

▶ Tori counters uke's hip throw, e.g. harai-goshi, by pushing his hips forward and lowering his centre of gravity. Tori grabs uke's waist with his left hand and lifts uke into the air by straightening his body. With uke in the air, tori swings uke over his left hip and finishes with a hip throw. (Pictures 1–3.) In a variation of utsuri-goshi, tori swings the left leg up during the throwing phase (Picture 4).

TAI-OTOSHI · UKI-OTOSHI
SUMI-OTOSHI · KATA-GURUMA

TAI-OTOSHI – BODY DROP

▶ Tori is in the correct natural posture (migi shizentai). Tori makes kuzushi diagonally upwards. Tori pivots on the ball of his right foot and straightens his body. The left foot comes close to his right at an angle of about 45 degrees to uke's feet. Tori moves his right foot keeping it low to the front of uke's right foot. Tori finishes the throw with a full body twist and a lift to the right after the body drop.

▶ Tai-otoshi requires good timing and seamless interaction of arms, legs and body forces.

TAI-OTOSHI GRIPS (KUMIKATA)

Tori's right hand is on uke's neck and left hand on the cuff of the right sleeve

Tori's right hand on uke's back and left hand on uke's right sleeve

Tori's left hand is on uke's right lapel from above or below his arm and his right hand is on uke's left lapel

PREPARATORY ACTIONS (TSUKURI) FOR TAI-OTOSHI

Tori presses down – pulls

Tori pushes – pulls

Tori's right hand pushes uke diagonally backwards and left hand pulls – both hands pull forward

VARIATIONS AND SITUATIONS FOR APPLYING TAI-OTOSHI

Tai-otoshi variation, defensive stance (jigotai)

▶ Tori's opening and kuzushi is done with hands up and forward. After the turn, tori's feet are parallel to uke's feet. The variation is also done by tori dropping his left knee to the mat.

Tai-otoshi variation, when uke is moving sideways

▶ Tori does kuzushi as uke moves sideways, so that uke's balance shifts completely to his right foot. Tori shifts his right foot to block uke's right foot, after which tori throws uke straight to the side or diagonally to the front.

Tai-otoshi variation, turning (mawari)

▶ Tori makes kuzushi to hidari side as if doing a throw to the left. Tori steps with his left foot in front of uke's left foot, pivots on his left foot to the right and simultaneously changes the direction of the hands to the right. Tori finishes the throw (kake) diagonally to the right front.

Tai-otoshi, tori stepping back

▶ Uke steps forward with his right foot. Tori retreats with left foot straight back with a long step and pulls uke down hard as in uki-otoshi. Tori moves his right foot to the side of uke's right ankle and finishes the throw (kake) to the side or diagonally to the front.

Tai-otoshi, when uke circles around clockwise

▶ Uke circles clockwise around. Tori uses his right hand to pull uke towards him while moving his left foot behind his right foot. Tori pulls uke with his left hand and with his right hand pushes to the right while moving his right foot in front of uke's right foot and twisting his body throws uke.

Combination feint o-uchi-gari – tai-otoshi

▶ Tori enters o-uchi-gari. Tori leaves his weight on his left foot, allowing his right foot to make a feinting motion to uke's left foot. Uke reacts by lifting his left foot up. Tori moves his right foot in front of uke's right foot and completes the throw (kake).

Combination o-uchi-gari – tai-otoshi

▶ Tori makes an o-uchi-gari, which uke counters by lifting his left foot up. Tori changes the throwing direction and pulls uke diagonally to the right front with his hands, stepping at the same time with his left foot behind his right foot, and then moving his right foot in front of uke's right foot and finishing the throw (kake).

Combination ko-uchi-gari – tai-otoshi

▶ Tori performs ko-uchi-gari, which uke counters by lifting his right leg up and stepping it back. Tori follows the direction of uke's movement. Tori steps his left foot behind his right foot and pushes uke diagonally back to the right. Tori moves his right foot in front of uke's right foot and throws uke forward.

Combination hidari ko-soto-gari/hidari de-ashi-harai – tai-otoshi

▶ Uke counters tori's hidari ko-soto-gari/hidari de-ashi-harai by lifting his left foot up and stepping it back. Tori changes the throwing direction to the right and moves his right foot in front of uke's right foot and finishes the throw (kake).

Combination feint hidari de-ashi-harai – tai-otoshi

▶ Tori taps uke's left leg with his right foot as if doing de-ashi-harai. Tori continues to move his right foot and moves it in front of uke's right foot and finishes the throw (kake).

Tai-otoshi with a sode-tsurikomi grip

▶ For example, in a starting situation, before tori and uke have both grips, tori grabs the cuff of uke's left sleeve with his right hand (sode-tsurikomi grip). Tori makes a tai-otoshi opening and kuzushi diagonally to the right front and throws uke straight in front of him.

Tai-otoshi with same-sided grip/combination o-soto-gari – tai-otoshi

▶ Tori has a grip on uke's right sleeve and right lapel. Tori makes kuzushi to the side or diagonally to the right front with his left hand pulling and his right hand against uke's chest pushing uke upwards. Tori does tai-otoshi in one step by moving his right foot directly to block uke's right foot. In o-soto-gari – tai-otoshi combination, tori's right foot is at uke's knee bend. Tori drops his foot down before finishing the throw to the side or diagonally to the front.

Tai-otoshi on uke's wrong foot

▶ In a situation where tori is having difficulty entering through uke's strong hand grip, tori will do a tai-otoshi from the side to uke's left foot. Tori places his right foot in front of uke's left foot during the throwing phase (kake) or into a contact with the inside of uke's left foot. Tori starts the throw with a forward kuzushi and enters with a 180-degree tai-sabaki. Tori throws uke in front of him. The throw requires strong hand movement and body rotation.

Tai-otoshi kaeshi-waza (sukashi) to uke's uchi-mata

▶ Uke enters to an hidari uchi-mata. At the point where uke has begun the foot swing, tori counters the throw with his hands and body. Tori moves his right foot in front of uke's right foot and finishes the throw (kake) with a body drop.

TAI-OTOSHI EXERCISES

Isometric training with belt, see page 33

Tandoku-renshu with bands

Chase, repeated attempts until uke is thrown.

COMBINATIONS FOLLOWING TAI-OTOSHI

- ▶ sasae-tsurikomi-ashi, page 56
- ▶ o-uchi-gari
- ▶ ko-uchi-gari, page 63
- ▶ uchi-mata, page 128
- ▶ tomoe-nage
- ▶ kesa-gatame, page 154
- ▶ juji-gatame, page 166

COUNTER-THROWS (KAESHI-WAZA) TO TAI-OTOSHI

- ▶ de-ashi-harai
- ▶ o-soto-gari
- ▶ ko-soto-gari, page 74
- ▶ yoko-tomoe-nage, page 142

UKI-OTOSHI – FLOATING DROP

▶ Uke steps forward with his right foot. Tori pulls uke strongly off balance and at the same time retreats with his left foot. Tori throws uke by pulling diagonally down hard.

SUMI-OTOSHI – CORNER DROP

▶ Uke steps forward. Tori breaks uke's balance backwards so that uke's body weight shifts to his right heel. Tori throws uke backwards with a hand throw, taking advantage of the right timing by pushing uke straight down with his hands.

KATA-GURUMA (VARIATION) – SHOULDER WHEEL

▶ Tori pulls uke up behind his neck, then rolls uke down. Kata-guruma is also done by going down on one or both knees. Grabbing the opponent's legs may be restricted by competition rules.

MOROTE-SEOI-NAGE · KATA-ERI-SEOI-NAGE

KATA-SODE-SEOI-NAGE · SEOI-OTOSHI · WAKI-OTOSHI

IPPON-SEOI-NAGE · (IPPON-)SEOI-OTOSHI

MOROTE-SEOI-NAGE – TWO-HANDED SHOULDER THROW

▶ Tori pulls uke up and forward with his hands. Then he twists and folds his right arm under uke's arm. At the same time, tori steps forward with his right foot (step 1) in front of uke and between his legs. Tori's right hand lifts uke up. Tori steps with his left foot (step 2) in front of uke's left foot, moves his right foot (step 3) in front of uke's right foot and pushes his elbow firmly into uke's armpit. Tori squats down with his back straight in front of uke. Tori pulls uke onto his back. Tori finishes the throw (kake) by straightening his legs and leaning forward.

MOROTE-SEOI-NAGE GRIPS (KUMIKATA)

Tori's left hand is on uke's lower sleeve

Tori's left hand is on uke's right lapel from the top of uke's hand

Tori's hands are on uke's lapels

PREPARATORY ACTIONS (TSUKURI) FOR MOROTE-SEOI-NAGE

Tori presses down – lifts up

Tori pushes – pulls

Tori's left hand pushes first to the right and then pulls to the left

Tori pulls with right hand right – left

Tori lifts uke up

DIFFERENT WAYS OF FINISHING MOROTE-SEOI-NAGE

Tori follows uke down to the mat   At the end, tori swings his right leg up

VARIATIONS AND SITUATIONS FOR APPLYING MOROTE-SEOI-NAGE

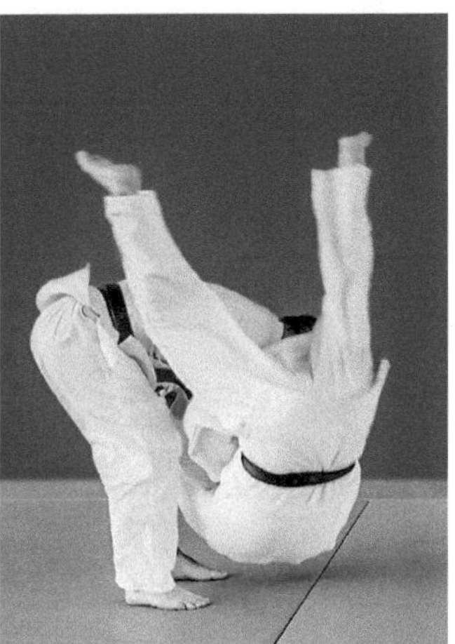

Morote-seoi-nage when tori retreats
▶ Uke steps forward with his right foot. After tori's kuzushi, tori jumps with his right foot in
  between uke's legs and pulls uke into contact with him. Tori finishes with a morote-seoi-nage.

Morote-seoi-nage, uke stepping forward-tori coming towards him

▶ Uke steps forward with his right foot. Tori pulls uke and ducks in with his right foot in front between uke's legs. Tori straightens his legs, leans forward and throws uke with speed.

Morote-seoi-nage to the side

▶ Tori and uke have a kenka-yotsu stance. Tori takes a long step with his left foot to the front of uke's right foot. The right foot follows alongside the left foot. Tori finishes the throw to the side or diagonally to the front.

Morote-seoi-nage with hands on uke's lower sleeves (variation of morote-seoi-nage)

▶ Tori takes the grip (kumikata) of uke's sleeves, for example in the starting situation. Tori can do morote-seoi-nage on either side.

KATA-ERI-SEOI-NAGE — single lapel shoulder throw (variation of morote-seoi-nage)

▶ Tori's grip (kumikata) is from uke's right sleeve and the same side lapel. During the entry phase, tori can also move his right foot next to uke's right ankle, then the throw is finished diagonally to the front right.

KATA-SODE-SEOI-NAGE (1) — single sleeve shoulder throw (variation of morote-seoi-nage)

▶ Tori grabs uke's right cuff with his left hand and with his right hand he grabs uke's sleeve from the same point from the inside. Tori pulls uke's right hand tight against his chest before finishing the throw. Tori may also place his right foot on the side of uke's right ankle, Picture 4.

KATA-SODE-SEOI-NAGE (2) — single sleeve shoulder throw (variation of morote-seoi-nage)

▶ Tori has a left hand grip on uke's right sleeve. Uke prevents tori from taking a right hand grip. Tori prepares the throw by pushing uke's right arm to the right before the kuzushi. Tori takes a right hand grip on uke's right biceps. Tori finishes with a morote-seoi-nage after getting both hands on uke's right hand.

Variation of morote-seoi-nage, with tori's hands on uke's left lapel

▶ For example, tori has both hands on uke's left collar at the start, and turns it into a morote-seoi-nage. In the kake phase of the throw, tori strongly twists his body to the left and, depending on the situation, follows uke to the mat.

SEOI-OTOSHI (1) – shoulder drop with one knee on the ground (variation of morote-seoi-nage)

▶ On entry, tori kneels with the right foot so that his right foot comes next to or between uke's right foot.

SEOI-OTOSHI (2) – shoulder drop with both knees on the ground (variation of morote-seoi-nage)

▶ On entry, tori jumps in front of or between uke's legs, then tori throws uke over his shoulder. In the kake phase, tori gains extra power by standing up with one or both legs (if there is a lift then the throw is no longer otoshi).

Combination o-soto-gari – morote-seoi-otoshi

▶ Uke blocks tori's o-soto-gari. Tori drops his right foot next to uke's right foot, turns forward and throws a morote-seoi-otoshi diagonally to the front.

Combination ko-soto-gari – morote-seoi-nage

▶ Uke counters a ko-soto-gari by lifting his right foot up. Tori puts his left foot down and with his right foot in front pivots to the right. Tori makes upper arm contact and finishes with a morote-seoi-nage.

Combination o-uchi-gari – morote-seoi-nage

▶ Uke counters tori's o-uchi-gari by lifting his left leg up and stepping it back. Tori steps his right foot in front of uke's right foot and moves his left foot in front of uke's left foot. Tori makes upper arm contact and finishes the throw.

Combination ko-uchi-gari – morote-seoi-nage

▶ Uke counters tori's ko-uchi-gari or feint of ko-uchi-gari by lifting his right foot up and stepping it back. Tori enters morote-seoi-nage with his right foot in front and finishes the throw diagonally to the right front.

Combination hidari sasae-tsurikomi-ashi – morote-seoi-nage

▶ Uke counters tori's hidari sasae-tsurikomi-ashi by stepping over tori's right foot with his left foot. Tori enters morote-seoi-nage right foot first and finishes the throw diagonally to the right front.

Morote-seoi-nage kaeshi-waza to uke's o-soto-gari

▶ Uke makes an o-soto-gari. Tori blocks it and pivots in front of uke, crouches and throws uke with morote-seoi-nage over his shoulders.

MOROTE-SEOI-NAGE EXERCISES

Solo training with bands

Carrying uke on the back

Squats with uke on the back

Rising from the knees

COMBINATIONS FOLLOWING MOROTE-SEOI-NAGE

- ▶ o-uchi-gari, page 71
- ▶ ko-uchi-gari, page 61
- ▶ o-soto-gari, page 82
- ▶ waki-otoshi

COUNTER-THROWS (KAESHI-WAZA) TO MOROTE-SEOI-NAGE

- ▶ ko-soto-gari uchi-mata, page 129
- ▶ ushiro-goshi
- ▶ tani-otoshi
- ▶ tomoe-nage

WAKI-OTOSHI (SUKUI-NAGE) – ARMPIT DROP

IPPON-SEOI-NAGE – ONE-ARM SHOULDER THROW

▶ Tori pulls uke up forward with his left hand and his right hand lifts uke. At the same time, tori steps forward with his right foot (step 1) in front of uke in the middle of his feet. Tori swings his right arm under uke's armpit and wraps it around uke's arm. Tori places his left foot (step 2) in front of uke's left foot and his right foot (step 3) in front of uke's right foot. Tori enters with his back straight and pulls uke onto his back. Facing forward, tori lowers himself below uke's centre of gravity, straightens his legs and throws uke forward by leaning forward.

IPPON-SEOI-NAGE GRIPS

Basic grip, right hand fingers
are turned inwards

Tori's left hand is on top of uke's
right hand from his collar

Tori's left hand is in uke's armpit

PREPARATORY ACTIONS (TSUKURI) FOR IPPON-SEOI-NAGE

Tori pushes down – lifts uke up

Tori pushes – pulls uke to
the right – to the left

Tori lifts uke up

WAYS OF FINISHING IPPON-SEOI-NAGE (KAKE)

Tori follows uke onto the mat

Tori's leg swings up at the end

Ippon seoi-nage with two steps forward

▶ After the kuzushi, tori steps his right foot in front of uke's right foot and his left foot in front of uke's left foot. Tori finishes with an ippon-seoi-nage.

Ippon-seoi-nage when uke advancing – tori comes towards him

▶ Uke advances with his right foot. Tori pulls uke towards him. Tori jumps in right foot first and crouches between uke's legs. Tori straightens his legs, leans forward and throws uke.

Ippon-seoi-nage to the side

▶ Tori takes a long step with his left foot in front of uke's right foot. His right foot follows alongside his left foot. Tori finishes with an ippon-seoi-nage to the side or diagonally to the front.

Ippon-seoi-nage when tori retreats

▶ Uke steps forward with his right foot. After kuzushi, tori pivots on his right foot with a 90-degree tai-sabaki in front of uke's left foot. Tori finishes the ippon-seoi-nage.

Ippon-seoi-nage, with uke's left hand clasped between tori and uke

▶ Uke has a left hand grip on tori's right sleeve. Tori moves his right arm to uke's right armpit and at the same time clasps uke's left arm as well. Tori finishes with an ippon-seoi-nage.

Ippon-seoi-nage, tori swinging his right leg and rolling onto the mat

▶ At the end of the ippon-seoi-nage (kake), tori releases his right foot from the mat and swings it upwards. Depending on the situation, tori may follow uke to the mat.

Ippon-seoi-nage, sweep with tori's right leg

▶ Uke counters tori's ippon-seoi-nage by stepping past tori to his right. Tori lifts his right foot off the ground and uses it to sweep uke's right foot from the outside.

Ippon-seoi-nage, with tori's right leg on the outside of uke's right leg or between his legs

▶ Tori comes between uke's legs with his right foot in front. Tori brings his right hand under uke's right armpit. His left foot follows next to his right foot. Tori's left foot is already turned into the direction of the throw. Tori moves his right leg deep next to or between uke's right leg. Tori throws uke over his shoulder diagonally to the right front by lifting his body up and leaning forward.

SEOI-OTOSHI (1) – one-arm shoulder drop
with one knee on the ground (ippon-seoi-nage hand grip)

▶ On entry, tori puts his right knee on the mat between uke's legs or outside his right leg. Tori leans forward and throws uke over his shoulder diagonally to the front.

SEOI-OTOSHI (2) – one-arm one arm shoulder throw
with both feet on the ground (ippon-seoi-nage hand grip)

▶ In the entry phase, tori jumps onto his knees in front of uke or between his legs. Tori throws uke over his shoulder straight to the front. Tori can add extra power to the throw by standing up with one or both legs before the final stage of the throw (kake). Then the throw is ippon-seoi-nage.

Ippon-seoi-nage after tori blocks uke's left hand grip

▶ Tori uses his right hand to block uke's left hand grip at the start. Tori immediately throws ippon-seoi-nage to his right side.

Combination ko-uchi-gari – hidari ippon-seoi-nage

▶ Tori makes a ko-uchi-gari or feint of ko-uchi-gari on uke's right foot. Uke counters the throw by lifting his right foot. Tori reverses the direction of the throw and finishes with a hidari ippon-seoi-nage. Depending on the situation, tori may also throw ippon-seoi- nage to the right side.

Combination o-uchi-gari – hidari ippon-seoi-nage (1)

▶ Tori does migi o-uchi-gari. Uke counters it by lifting his left foot up and stepping it backwards. Tori pivots on his right foot to the left and finishes with hidari ippon-seoi-nage to the side.

Combination o-uchi-gari – ippon-seoi-nage (2)

▶ Tori does o-uchi-gari or feint of o-uchi-gari. Uke counters by lifting his left foot up and stepping it backwards. After kuzushi, tori pivots on his right foot and does with his left foot tai-sabaki in front of uke's left foot and finishes with ippon-seoi-nage.

Combination o-soto-gari – hidari ippon-seoi-nage

▶ Tori does o-soto-gari. Uke counters by shifting body weight to his left foot. Tori reverses the throw to the left side and does hidari ippon-seoi-nage.

IPPON-SEOI-NAGE EXERCISES

One-on-one training with bands

Carrying uke on your back

Squatting with uke on the back

Rising from the knees

COMBINATIONS FOLLOWING IPPON-SEOI-NAGE

- ▶ o-uchi-gari
- ▶ ko-uchi-gari, page 63
- ▶ o-soto-gari, page 82
- ▶ waki-otoshi
- ▶ sumi-gaeshi
- ▶ ushiro-kesa-gatame/yoko-shiho-gatame, page 154
- ▶ juji-gatame

COUNTER-THROWS (KAESHI-WAZA) TO IPPON-SEOI-NAGE

- ▶ ko-soto-gari
- ▶ ushiro-goshi
- ▶ tani-otoshi
- ▶ tomoe-nage, page 142

UCHI-MATA · UCHI-MATA-MAKIKOMI · UCHI-MATA-GAESHI
UCHI-MATA-SUKASHI · HARAI-GOSHI · HARAI-MAKIKOMI
HANE-GOSHI · HANE-MAKIKOMI
ASHI-GURUMA · O-GURUMA · SOTO-MAKIKOMI

▶ Depending on how uchi-mata is done, it is classified as either a leg or hip throw. It is sometimes difficult to draw the line. Uchi-mata is shown below as a leg throw and, from page 130 onwards, as a hip throw.

UCHI-MATA – ASHI-WAZA (nage-no-kata style)

▶ Tori makes kuzushi diagonally to the front so that uke rises on balls of his feet. Tori enters with his right side towards uke. Tori steps in front of uke with his right foot and his left foot follows in front of uke's left foot. Tori's left foot points to the front right. Tori throws uke by sweeping with the back of his right thigh on the inside of uke's left thigh.

UCHI-MATA GRIPS (KUMIKATA)

Tori's right hand is on uke's neck and his left hand is on uke's left lower sleeve	Tori's elbow is high and the hand is pushing uke by the chin	Tori's right hand is on uke's right collar	Tori's right hand is on uke's left shoulder

Tor's right hand is around uke's neck	Tori's right hand is on uke's back/waist under his left arm	Tori's right hand is on uke's belt over his left arm

PREPARATORY ACTIONS, followed by uke's counter-reaction and tori's attack

Tori presses down and lifts

Tori pushes and pulls

Tori lifts

Tori steps forward, returns to base position and attacks

Tori pushes, pulls, pushes... with both hands

Tori takes dance steps

VARIATIONS AND SITUATIONS FOR APPLYING UCHI-MATA ASHI-WAZA

Variation of uchi-mata with ken-ken, that is, jumping

▶ Ken-ken uchi-mata is often done from a kenka-yotsu situation. Tori makes kuzushi in the direction of uke's right foot toes. Tori's left foot comes in front or to the side of uke's left foot. Tori continues to pull with his hands, twisting to the left. Tori's right leg sweep comes to the height of the knee of uke's left leg. Tori continues the throw by hopping forward with his left foot or circling to the right. Tori pulls down uke with his left hand and pushes with his right hand.

Combination (1) hidari de-ashi-harai – uchi-mata

▶ Tori does hidari de-ashi-harai attempts on uke's left foot. Uke anticipates tori's de-ashi-harai and steps back with his left foot. Tori enters on his right supporting leg and finishes the uchi-mata.

Combination (2) hidari de-ashi-harai – uchi-mata

▶ Tori makes a feint with his right foot on uke's left leg and comes in with a jump into the uchi-mata.

Combination (1) sasae-tsurikomi-ashi – uchi-mata

▶ Uke counters tori's sasae-tsurikomi-ashi by stepping over tori's left leg with his right leg. Tori quickly pivots on his right foot with a 180 degree tai-sabaki in front of uke. Tori finishes the uchi-mata with a sweep of his right leg onto uke's left leg.

Combination (2) sasae-tsurikomi-ashi – hidari uchi-mata

▶ Uke counters tori's sasae-tsurikomi-ashi by stepping over tori's left leg with his right leg. Tori reverses the throw to hidari. Tori enters uchi-mata with his left foot in front. Tori finishes the uchi-mata with his left leg sweep to uke's right leg.

Combination ko-uchi-gari – uchi-mata

▶ Uke counters ko-uchi-gari by lifting his right foot up and stepping it back. Tori lifts and pulls uke diagonally forward and enters uchi-mata on his right supporting leg. Tori finishes with a throw to uke's left leg.

Combination (1) o-uchi-gari – uchi-mata

▶ Uke counters tori's o-uchi-gari by lifting his left leg up. Tori jumps between uke's legs with his left foot and does a leg sweep to uke's left thigh.

Combination (2) o-uchi-gari – uchi-mata

▶ Uke counters tori's o-uchi-gari with his body. Tori keeps his leg bent behind uke's right knee. Tori changes the throwing direction to the front and continues the movement with a ken-ken uchi-mata.

Combination tai-otoshi – uchi-mata

▶ Uke counters tori's tai-otoshi by stepping over tori's right leg with his right leg or anticipates tori's tai-otoshi on the entry phase with his left foot step forward. Tori enters uchi-mata on his right supporting leg and does a sweep to uke's left thigh.

Uchi-mata as uke stands up from a kneeling position

▶ Uke has his right knee on the mat. Tori uses his hands to lift uke up. As uke's right knee rises, tori enters uchi-mata and finishes the throw on uke's left leg. Tori can also do uchi-mata to hidari, in which case the sweep comes to uke's right leg.

Uchi-mata kaeshi-waza to uke's morote-seoi-otoshi

▶ Tori counters uke's morote-seoi-otoshi by stepping his right foot in front of uke. Tori's left foot goes between uke's legs and right hand pulls forward and left hand pushes to the side. Tori finishes with a hidari-uchi-mata sweeping uke's right leg.

Variation of the uchi-mata turning (mawari)

▶ Tori steps with his left foot in front of uke's left foot and simultaneously makes kuzushi to the right. Tori pivots or jumps on his left foot between uke's legs and finishes the throw.

UCHI-MATA – KOSHI-WAZA

▶ Tori makes kuzushi diagonally forward while his right hand controls uke's head. Tori steps forward with his right foot and his left foot immediately follows between uke's legs to the same line. The sole of tori's supporting leg is firmly planted on the mat. Tori makes full body contact with uke from the hip up and swings his right leg between uke's legs or to his right inner thigh. At the same time, tori leans his body forward to a horizontal position, causing uke to follow tori's body movement and be thrown to tori's side. Tori's eyes and head follow where uke is thrown.

VARIATIONS AND SITUATIONS FOR APPLYING UCHI-MATA KOSHI-WAZA

Uchi-mata side forward

▶ Tori steps his right foot sideways directly between uke's legs. His left foot follows and steps next to his right foot. Tori turns his body. Right leg sweeps between uke's legs or inside his right thigh. The entry of tori's left foot and the sweep of his right leg occur almost simultaneously.

Variation of uchi-mata tobi-komi

▶ Tori and uke are in a kenka-yotsu stance. Tori makes a kuzushi in the direction of uke's toes. Tori enters between uke's legs with a long jump of his left foot with the foot already turned forwards. Tori sweeps his right leg into uke's right inner thigh. Tori's sweeping leg controls the movement of the final phase of the throw (kake). Tori's gaze is turned to the point of uke's fall.

Uchi-mata with 180 degree tai-sabaki as uke advances

▶ Uke moves sideways to his right or forward with his right foot. Tori makes a quick 180 degree tai-sabaki on his right foot, almost on the spot, while making full body contact with uke. Tori sweeps with his right leg to the inside of uke's right or left thigh, depending on uke's position.

Combination feint o-soto-gari – uchi-mata

▶ Tori steps forward with his left foot and his right knee follows the movement as if he is doing an o-soto-gari. Uke moves into a defensive stance. Tori jumps on his left foot between uke's legs and finishes uchi-mata.

Uchi-mata kaeshi-waza to uke's o-uchi-gari

▶ Tori counters uke's o-uchi-gari by lifting his leg over. Tori turns 180 degrees with a tai-sabaki in front of uke and finishes uchi-mata.

UCHI-MATA-MAKIKOMI – inner thigh -wrap-up throw to the mat (yoko-sutemi-waza)

▶ After tori's uchi-mata sweep, the movement is stopped due to uke's block. Tori releases his right hand grip on the lapel and moves his hand over uke's head. Tori dives to the mat with his right hand in front of him, followed by uke. The throw is often made from a starting position when tori and uke have only a one-handed grip.

UCHI-MATA EXERCISES

Solo practice (tandoku-renshu) with different variations of uchi-mata and from different situations

Jumping exercises on the supporting leg alone and with uke

Three person uchi-komi (power uchi-komi)

COMBINATIONS FOLLOWING UCHI-MATA

- ▶ de-ashi-harai, page 48
- ▶ ko-uchi-gari, page 62
- ▶ o-uchi-gari, page 70
- ▶ o-soto-gari, page 81
- ▶ ko-soto-gake
- ▶ tai-otoshi
- ▶ tomoe-nage, page 144
- ▶ tani-otoshi

COUNTER-THROWS (KAESHI-WAZA) TO UCHI-MATA

- ▶ de-ashi-harai, page 50
- ▶ ko-soto-gake
- ▶ uchi-mata-gaeshi, page 134
- ▶ uchi-mata sukashi/tai-otoshi, page 134
- ▶ tani-otoshi ura-nage, page 146

UCHI-MATA-GAESHI – uchi-mata counter-throw

UCHI-MATA-SUKASHI – uchi-mata side step (te-waza)/TAI-OTOSHI

HARAI-GOSHI – HIP SWEEP

▶ After kuzushi, tori steps his right foot in front of uke's feet and his left foot follows with the sole of the foot firmly on the tatami and he takes full body contact. Tori rotates uke's body strongly to the right and simultaneously sweeps with a strong swing of his right leg above uke's right knee.

HARAI-GOSHI GRIPS (KUMIKATA)

   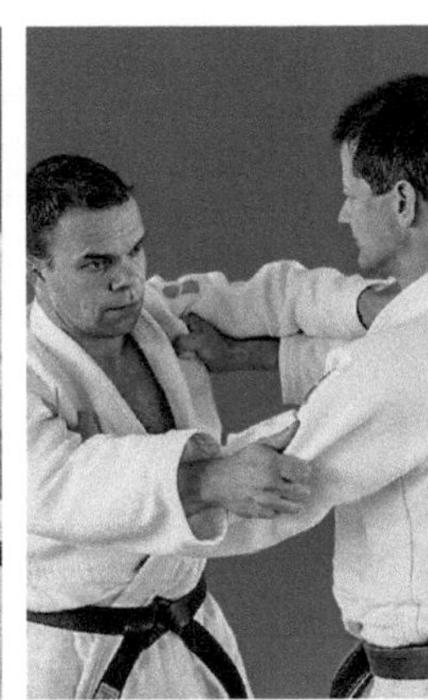 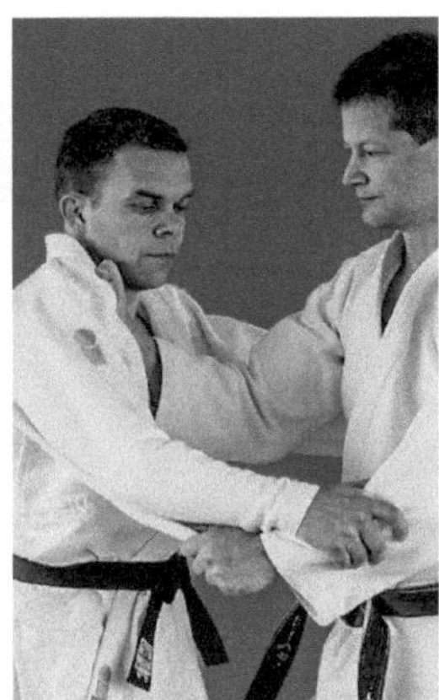

Right hand under uke's armpit

Right hand on uke's belt from front, back and side

Right hand on uke's neck

Both hands under uke's armpits

Yama-arashi -grip

VARIATIONS AND SITUATIONS FOR APPLYING HARAI-GOSHI

Harai-goshi turning (mawari)

▶ Tori breaks uke's balance to the left and steps his left foot in front of uke's left foot. As uke reacts to the right, tori pivots on his left foot to the right and finishes the throw.

Harai-goshi – uke moves his head under tori's arm

▶ Uke prevents tori from getting a right hand grip. After tori gets the grip, uke dives his head under tori's right hand. Tori immediately jumps into the harai-goshi with a strong twist of his body. Tori follows uke to the mat.

Combination hidari de-ashi-harai/hidari ko-soto-gari – harai-goshi

▶ Tori does hidari de-ashi-harai or ko-soto-gari. Uke counters the throw by moving his left foot back. Tori jumps around on the ball of his left foot and finishes the throw.

HARAI-MAKIKOMI – hip sweep wraparound throw to the mat (yoko-sutemi-waza)

▶ In the sweeping phase tori lifts his right arm over uke's head and takes uke's right arm under his armpit. Tori drops down onto his right arm, with uke following him to his right side.

HANE-GOSHI–HIP SPRING

▶ Tori takes a tight upper body and side contact to uke. Tori bounces upwards with his right
leg bent against the inside of uke's right leg. Tori finishes the throw to the side.

HANE-MAKIKOMI–springing wraparound throw to the mat (yoko-sutemi-waza)

▶ After a failed hane-goshi, tori takes his right hand over uke's head and falls with
his right hand in front to the mat, and uke follows tori onto the mat.

ASHI-GURUMA–LEG WHEEL

▶ Tori makes kuzushi forward and steps forward with his right foot in front of uke and with his left foot in front of
or outside of uke's left foot. Tori places the calf of his stiffened extended right leg at uke's shin and throws uke to
the right in a twisting motion as if the extended leg were acting as an axle for a wheel. Ashi-guruma while turning
(mawari) is done with tori stepping with his left foot in front of uke's left foot and pivoting on it in front of uke.

Combination o-soto-gari – ashi-guruma

▶ Tori presses hard with his right leg on uke's right leg at the knee as if he is doing ken-ken o-soto-gari (jumping). Uke reacts and moves his body to the left. Tori reverses the throwing direction to forward ashi-guruma.

O-GURUMA – BIG WHEEL

▶ Tori breaks uke's balance forward and causes uke to move. Tori steps in front of uke with his right foot and in front of uke's left foot with his left foot. Tori places the thigh of his stiffly extended right leg above uke's knee and throws uke to the side as if the extended leg were an axle of a wheel. O-guruma can also done by turning (mawari) with tori stepping with his left foot in front of uke's left foot and using it to pivot in front of uke and finish the throw.

SOTO-MAKIKOMI – OUTER WRAPAROUND THROW TO THE MAT (YOKO-SUTE-MI-WAZA)

▶ For example, after an attempt of tsurikomi-goshi, tori presses uke's right arm against his chest and moves his right leg in front of uke's right leg. Tori rolls forward with his right foot on the mat and his right hand in front of him onto the mat, followed by uke. In contrast to soto-makikomi, in harai-makikomi tori sweeps uke's right leg.

TOMOE-NAGE · YOKO-TOMOE-NAGE · URA-NAGE
TANI-OTOSHI · YOKO-OTOSHI · SUMI-GAESHI · YOKO-GAKE
YOKO-WAKARE · YOKO-GURUMA · UKI-WAZA

TOMOE-NAGE – STOMACH THROW

▶ Tori lifts and pulls uke with both hands and at the same time steps between uke's legs with his left foot. Tori places the sole of his right foot on uke's lower abdomen. Tori pulls uke towards himself, drops to his back and extends right leg. Uke rolls over onto his back close to tori's head on the left side.

TOMOE-NAGE GRIPS (KUMIKATA)

Tori's left hand is on uke's right lapel	Tori's hands are on uke's sleeves	Tori's right hand is on uke's right cuff and his left hand is on uke's biceps	Tori's left hand is on uke's right sleeve and his right hand is on his lapel

PREPARATORY ACTIONS (TSUKURI) FOR TOMOE-NAGE

Tori pushes uke down – lifts up

Tori pushes – pulls uke

VARIATIONS AND SITUATIONS FOR APPLYING TOMOE-NAGE

   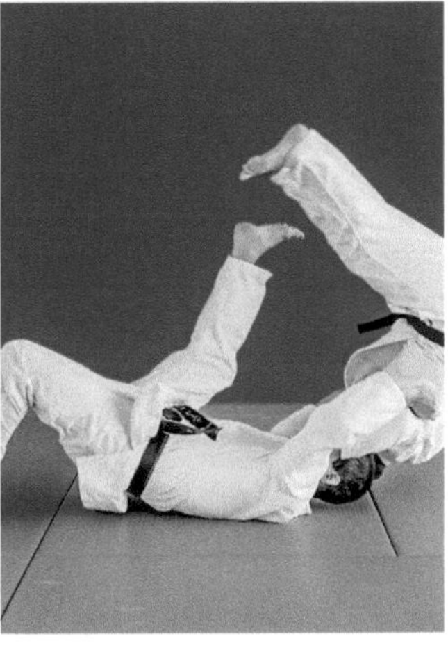

Tomoe-nage when uke steps forward

▶ Uke steps forward with his right foot. Tori pulls uke towards himself with his arms and body.
Tori places his right foot on uke's lower abdomen. Tori finishes the tomoe-nage by
extending his leg and pulling uke over his head with his hands.

   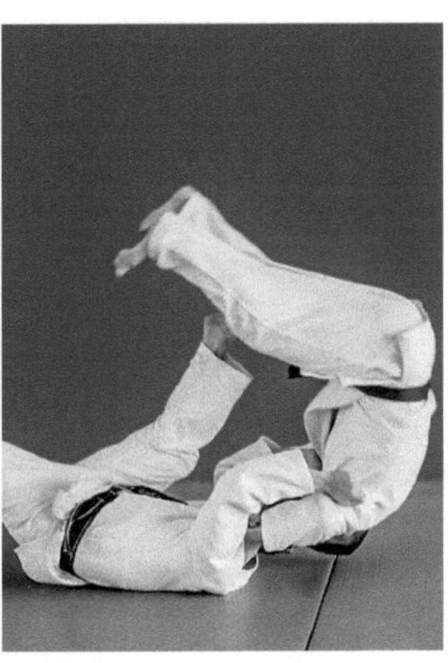

Tomoe-nage with a jump in

▶ Tori uses his hands to lift uke up and pulls towards himself (kuzushi). Tori jumps with his left foot deep between
uke's legs and places his right foot during the jump on uke's lower abdomen. Tori finishes (kake) the tomoe-nage.

Tomoe-nage when uke returns from a throw attempt

▶ Tori blocks uke's forward throw attempt, e.g. harai-goshi or seoi-nage. Uke is returning to starting position and turning to face tori. At the point when uke pulls his right foot further from tori, tori
makes kuzushi and places his right foot on uke's lower abdomen. Tori finishes the tomoe-nage.

YOKO-TOMOE-NAGE – side stomach throw, variation of tomoe-nage

▶ Tori breaks uke's balance to the right. Tori steps his left foot next to uke's right foot. Tori places his right foot on uke's lower abdomen. Tori drops onto his right side and rolls uke over to the right with his hands.

Combination feint o-soto-gari – yoko-tomoe-nage

▶ Tori steps with his left foot next to uke's right foot as if doing an o-soto-gari. Uke reacts by stepping backwards with his left foot. Standing on his right foot, tori places his left foot on uke's lower abdomen, and at the same time turns and drops to his left side. Tori completes the yoko-tomoe-nage.

Yoko-tomoe-nage kaeshi-waza tai-otoshi/ippon-seoi-nage

▶ Tori counters uke's tai-otoshi or ippon-seoi-nage by jumping over with his right foot. Tori turns his body to the right, places his left foot on uke's lower abdomen, drops down and finishes with yoko-tomoe-nage to the left.

Yoko-tomoe-nage kaeshi-waza to ko-uchi-gari

▶ Tori counters uke's ko-uchi-gari by lifting his right foot up and stepping it backwards. Tori places his left foot on uke's lower abdomen and finishes with a yoko-tomoe-nage to the left.

Combination ko-uchi-gari – yoko-tomoe-nage

▶ Uke counters tori's ko-uchi-gari by lifting his foot up and stepping it back. Tori places his left foot on uke's lower abdomen. Tori finishes with a yoko-tomoe-nage to the left.

Combination o-uchi-gari – yoko-tomoe-nage

▶ Uke counters tori's o-uchi-gari by stepping back with his left foot. Tori is standing on his right foot and places his left foot on uke's lower abdomen. Tori finishes with a yoko-tomoe-nage to the left.

Combination uchi-mata – yoko-tomoe-nage

▶ Uke blocks tori's uchi-mata. Tori places his right, sweeping leg, toes pointing to the right, next to his own left foot and then lifts his left foot on uke's lower abdomen. Tori finishes with a yoko-tomoe-nage to the left.

Yoko-tomoe-nage with one-handed grip or yama-arashi grip

▶ Tori has his left hand on uke's right sleeve or, as in this picture an yama-arashi grip, on uke's right sleeve and right lapel. Tori pulls uke strongly forward. Tori steps his right foot in front of uke's left foot and place his left foot on uke's lower abdomen. Tori pulls uke down towards himself. Tori finishes with a yoko-tomoe-nage to the left.

Two feet variation of tomoe-nage

▶ Tori enters with his left foot and places his right foot on uke's lower abdomen. Tori drops to his back and places his left foot on uke's lower abdomen. Tori pulls uke down and finishes with a tomoe-nage to the left. Tori follows uke and moves into tate-shiho-gatame or kesa-gatame, for example.

TOMOE-NAGE EXERCISES

Tomoe-nage tandoku-renshu

Yoko-tomoe-nage tandoku-renshu

Entering jump into tomoe-nage

Double leg push   Single leg push

COMBINATIONS FOLLOWING TOMOE-NAGE
- juji-gatame, page 166
- tate-shiho-gatame, page 155
- kesa-gatame

URA-NAGE – REAR THROW

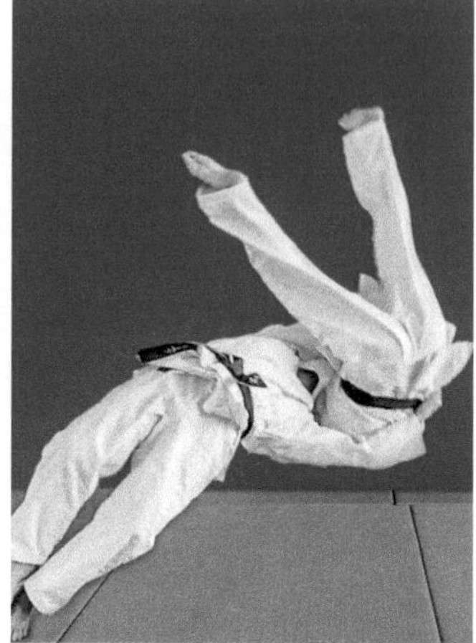

- Tori blocks uke's attempted throw, such as o-soto-gari, uchi-mata or harai-goshi. Tori drops his centre of gravity down by crouching below uke's centre of gravity. Tori ties uke to himself by grabbing uke around his waist. Tori throws uke over his left shoulder by straightening his legs, pushing his hips forward and throwing himself on his back.

Variation of ura-nage

- Tori blocks uke's throwing attempt with his hands and hips and by bending his legs. Tori pulls uke backwards with his hands. Tori lifts uke upwards with the inside of his left leg. Tori finishes the throw by arching himself backwards to the mat. Uke is thrown on his back next to tori.

TANI-OTOSHI – VALLEY DROP

▶ Tori makes kuzushi to uke's back right. Tori moves to uke's side and drops down on his left side with his left leg extended behind uke. Tori's right heel gives him support when uke is thrown backwards on his back.

Tani-otoshi from a jigotai

▶ Tori starts the throw with his left foot in front and moves it behind uke. Tori drops to his left side behind uke with his left leg outstretched. Tori finishes with a tani-otoshi. Combinations leading to tani-otoshi include o-soto-gari – tani-otoshi, ko-soto-gari – tani-otoshi and ippon-seoi-nage – hidari tani-otoshi. Combination of tani-otoshi – kuzure-yoko-shiho-gatame page 155.

YOKO-OTOSHI – SIDE DROP

▶ Tori prepares the throw (tsukuri) by pressing uke firmly to the right. As a reaction, uke shifts his weight to his left. Tori continues uke's movement and makes a kuzushi to the left so that uke's left foot is lifted up. Uke's balance is on the outside edge of his right foot. Tori drops to his left side with his left leg outstretched next to uke's right foot. Tori completes the throw by pulling uke down with his left hand and pushing with his right hand so that uke is thrown next to tori.

SUMI-GAESHI – CORNER THROW

- Uke is in a defensive stance. Tori drops to his back. Tori places the instep of his right foot on the inside thigh of uke's left foot. Tori throws uke over his right shoulder. Tori can grab uke's belt from the back with his right hand.
- Combination: ippon-seoi-nage – sumi-gaeshi; sumi-gaeshi – kuzure-tate-shiho-gatame page 156.

YOKO-GAKE – SIDE HOOK

- Tori uses both hands to break uke's balance to the left front. Tori places the sole of his left foot to the right side of uke's right ankle. Tori pulls uke firmly downwards and drops down onto his left side. Tori hooks uke's right foot upwards. Uke lands next to tori.

YOKO-WAKARE – SIDE SEPARATION

- Tori makes kuzushi forward. Tori straightens his right leg to uke's right side. Tori throws himself on his back. Uke is thrown over tori's right side.

YOKO-GURUMA – SIDE WHEEL

▶ Tori blocks uke's hip throw attempt and pulls uke into contact with him. Tori places his right leg between uke's legs. Tori drops to his left side and pulls uke along with him in a twisting motion.

UKI-WAZA – FLOATING THROW

▶ Tori makes kuzushi to the front right so that uke comes on the toes of his right foot. Tori falls to his left side with his left leg extended in front of uke's right foot, which prevents uke from advancing. Uke is thrown over tori's left shoulder.

KATAME-WAZA

OSAE-KOMI-WAZA

KESA-GATAME · KUZURE-KESA-GATAME · MAKURA-KESA-GATAME
USHIRO-KESA-GATAME · KATA-GATAME · KAMI-SHIHO-GATAME
KUZURE-KAMI-SHIHO-GATAME · YOKO-SHIHO-GATAME
KUZURE-YOKO-SHIHO-GATAME · TATE-SHIHO-GATAME
KUZURE-TATE-SHIHO-GATAME

KATAME-WAZA – CONTROL TECHNIQUES

INTRODUCTION

Control techniques are the hold downs (osae-komi-waza), armlocks (kansetsu-waza) and chokes (shime-waza).

- ▶ Current competition rules allow control techniques to be applied only in mat situations.
- ▶ In international competitions, quite a few ippons are done with katame-waza techniques and most of them with osae-komi-waza.
- ▶ The champion must be strong enough on the mat not to be afraid of going to the mat.
- ▶ The champion's tokui-waza system also includes katame-waza techniques.
- ▶ Control techniques and transitions to the control techniques should be practised in every training session.
- ▶ Control techniques are practised in the same way as throws, by doing numerous repetitions.
- ▶ The champion must know how to counter, dodge and escape from control techniques.
- ▶ Practising escapes is the best way to learn how to avoid being caught in a control technique.

OSAE-KOMI-WAZA – HOLD DOWNS

Tori controls uke in a hold down through a single point or several points of contact.
Tori's entire body from head to toe must be involved in the hold down.

KESA-GATAME – scarf hold
Combination to juji-gatame, page 167.

KUZURE-KESA-GATAME – a variation of scarf hold

MAKURA-KESA-GATAME – cushion scarf hold

USHIRO-KESA-GATAME – rear scarf hold
Tori's left hand is on uke's belt.

KATA-GATAME – shoulder holding

KAMI-SHIHO-GATAME –
top four-corner hold
Combination to juji-gatame, page 167

KUZURE-KAMI-SHIHO-GATAME –
variation of top four-corner hold

YOKO-SHIHO-GATAME –
side locking four-corner hold

KUZURE-YOKO-SHIHO-GATAME –
side locking four-corner hold variation

TATE-SHIHO-GATAME –
straight locking four-corner hold

KUZURE-TATE-SHIHO-GATAME – straight locking four-corner hold variations

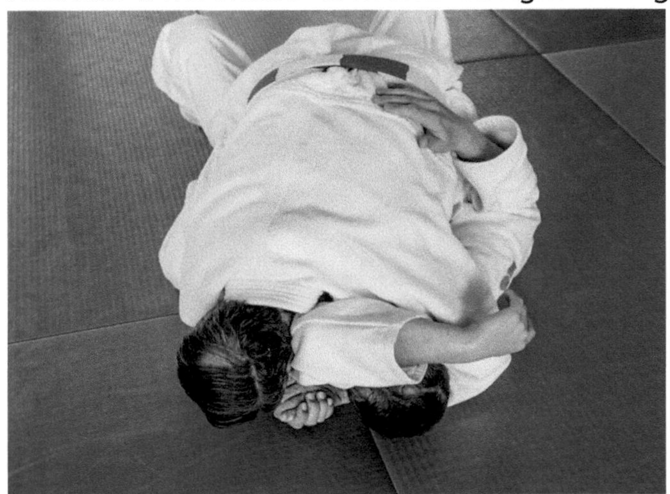

TRANSITION FROM THROWING (NAGE-WAZA) TO HOLD DOWN (OSAE-KOMI-WAZA)

- From any throw, you can move to some hold down.
- The transition to a hold down is reflexive.
- During the transition phase, tori controls uke with his hands, feet and body at all times.

DE-ASHI-HARAI – KESA-GATAME/YOKO-SHIHO-GATAME

   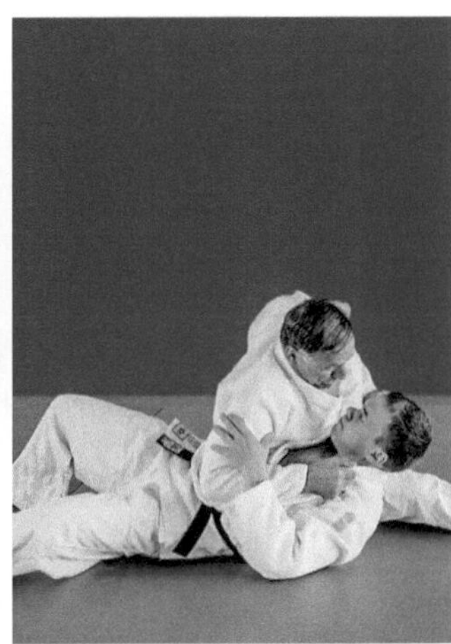

O-UCHI-GARI – KESA-GATAME

KO-UCHI-GARI – KESA-GATAME

TAI-OTOSHI – KESA-GATAME

IPPON-SEOI-NAGE – USHIRO-KESA-GATAME (YOKO-SHIHO-GATAME)

HARAI-TSURIKOMI-ASHI (SASAE-TSURIKOMI-ASHI) – KUZURE-YOKO-SHIHO-GATAME

TANI-OTOSHI – KUZURE YOKO-SHIHO-GATAME

TOMOE-NAGE – TATE-SHIHO-GATAME

TRANSITION ON THE MAT TO OSAE-KOMI-WAZA

▶ A transition from armlocks and some chokes to hold down can also be made.
▶ The main situations are 1. uke on his back, 2. uke on all fours, tori on his side, 3. uke on all fours, tori on top of uke, 4. uke on all fours, tori on the back of uke, and 5. tori on his back.
▶ There are several versions of each situation.
▶ The important thing is to know how to utilise the different situations.
▶ Below is an example of each of the main situations.

Uke is on his back and tori is between his legs

▶ Tori tries to get on either side of uke and from there into the hold down.
▶ Tori keeps his back as straight as possible and his head upright during the transition.
▶ Tori controls uke's legs with his hands and feet.
▶ Tori's toes are on the mat so that he can move quickly on them.

 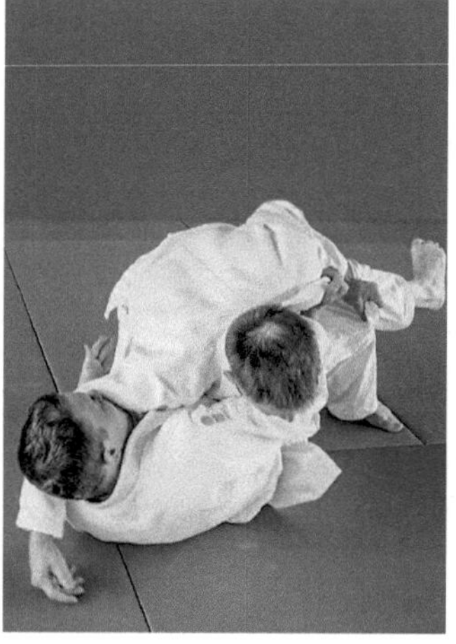  

Uke on all fours, tori on his side

- ▶ Tori takes hold with his left hand under uke's right armpit from his left lapel.
- ▶ Tori controls uke with his left side. Tori grabs uke's left sleeve with his right
  hand and turns uke on his back, then tori takes kesa-gatame.

Uke on all fours, tori on the side of uke's head

  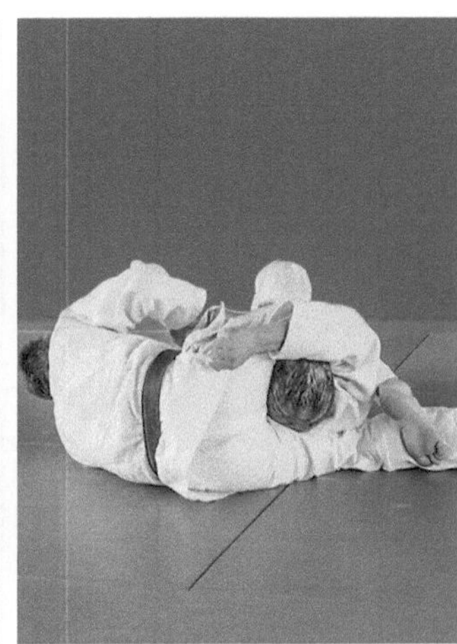 

- ▶ Tori hooks uke's right arm with his left leg and presses his right knee between uke's neck and left shoulder.
- ▶ Tori turns uke to the left by pulling up uke's left arm while crossing his legs as in sankaku-jime.
- ▶ Tori releases his right hand and turns on top of uke in kuzure-yoko-shiho-gatame.

Uke is on all fours, tori is on the side of uke's head

- Tori has a grip with both hands on uke's belt, left hand is under uke's right arm.
- Tori sits with his back straight next to uke and moves his right foot to uke's right thigh.
- Tori turns uke with his hands to the right and at the same time lifts uke with his right foot from his right thigh and pushes off with his left leg.
- As uke turns over on its back, tori moves into a hold down, such as kuzure-yoko-shiho-gatame.

Uke is on all fours, tori is on his back

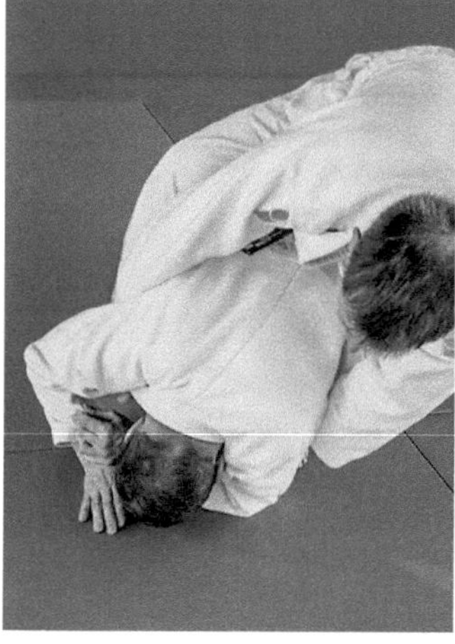 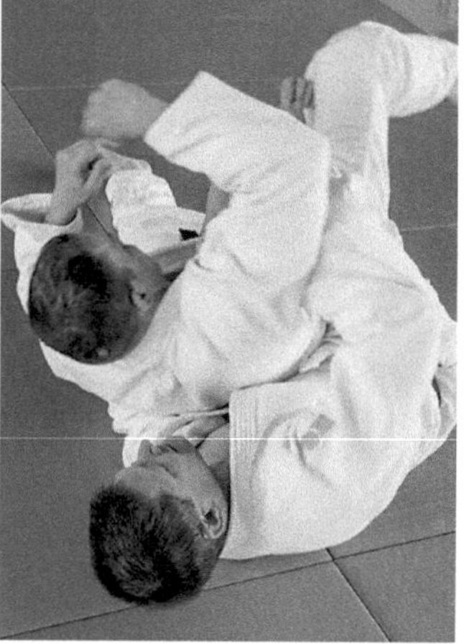  

- Tori takes grip with both hands on uke's lapels under his armpits and places his right foot at uke's knee and his left foot under uke.
- Tori throws himself to the left, taking uke with him. Tori moves out from underneath uke, catching uke in a kuzure-yoko-shiho-gatame.

Tori on his back, uke between his legs (1)

- ▶ Tori is on his back or throws himself under uke on his back while uke is on all fours. Tori grabs uke's right sleeve with his hands and presses it against his belly and moves his left leg between uke's legs.
- ▶ Tori rises up against uke, moves his left hand to uke's belt and lands on the mat. Tori moves his right hand from underneath uke to uke's belt and his right foot between uke's legs.
- ▶ Tori rolls uke to the left or right, leaving uke in a tight hold down.
- ▶ When practising the movement, progress systematically step by step.

Tori on his back, uke between his legs (2)

- ▶ Tori uses his left hand to move uke's right hand between his own arm and uke's head. Tori clasps his palms together behind uke's neck and holds uke tightly to him.
- ▶ Tori holds uke's legs by straightening his own legs around uke's legs at the thighs.
- ▶ Tori turns to the left and rolls uke on his back and stays in kata-gatame or kuzure-tate-shiho-gatame.

KANSETSU-WAZA

UDE-HISHIGI-UDE-GATAME · UDE-HISHIGI-HARA-GATAME
UDE-HISHIGI-WAKI-GATAME · UDE-HISHIGI-HIZA-GATAME
UDE-GARAMI · UDE-HISHIGI-JUJI-GATAME

KANSETSU-WAZA – ARMLOCKS

▶ Arm locks are made on uke's outstretched (usually gatame) or bent (garami=entwined) elbow.
▶ The armlocks require complete and continuous control of the opponent.

UDE-GATAME – arm crush armlock, tori rotates and pushes on uke's elbow

For example, an escape attempt from kuzure-kesa-gatame

WAKI-GATAME – armpit armlock, tori presses with his side on uke's arm and lifts it

HARA-GATAME – stomach armlock, tori presses uke's straight arm with his stomach at the elbow

HIZA-GATAME – knee lock, tori presses uke's outstretched arm at the elbow.

UDE-GARAMI – entangled armlock, uke lying on his back

Tori pushes uke's hand under his knee cap

For example, an escape attempt from kuzure-kesa-gatame

Tori presses uke's wrist into the mat with his right hand and lifts uke's elbow with his left hand

▶ Uke's left arm is hooked upwards. Tori grabs uke's wrist with his left hand and his own wrist under uke's arm with his right hand. Tori presses down on uke's wrist and lifts uke's elbow with his right hand.

UDE-GARAMI – entangled armlock, tori on his back

▶ Tori grabs uke's left wrist with right hand, pushes his left hand into uke's armpit and grabs his own wrist.
▶ Tori uses his right hand to push up uke's arm and finishes the armlock.

JUJI-GATAME – elbow crushing cross armlock

▶ Tori tightly controls uke's arm between his thighs before throwing himself onto his back with a ball-like movement.
▶ Tori's buttocks are attached to uke's side and uke's little finger points downwards. Tori lifts his hips and presses uke's hand firmly against himself.
▶ In the variation used in competitions, pictured right, tori crosses his legs.

Escape from juji-gatame

▶ Before the opponent has gained full control, tori (left picture) twists his body to the left and turns his right hand so that his little finger is pointing up.
▶ Tori grabs uke's ankle with his left hand and lifts it up, pulling his right hand towards himself.

JUJI-GATAME, SEPARATING UKE'S HANDS

"Pattern four". Tori's and uke's hands form a pattern resembling the number four

Tori swings from side to side

Tori's palms together

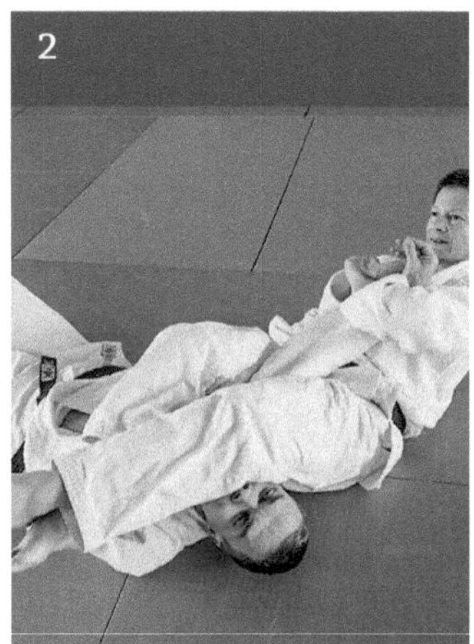

Tori rises up to a sitting position in between

Tori crosses his legs over uke's arms, pressing uke's arms down

VARIATIONS AND SITUATIONS FOR APPLYING JUJI-GATAME

Juji-gatame, tori on his back on the mat, uke between his legs

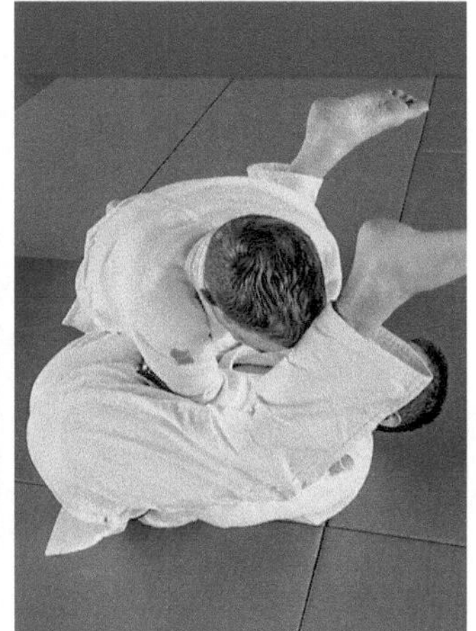

▶ Tori, lying on his back, turns his body to a 90 degree angle with a swinging motion to the right or by first grabbing the inside of uke's left knee bend with his right hand.
▶ Tori raises his left leg to uke's neck and presses uke to the mat.

Juji-gatame lying on the side, tori is on his back on the mat with uke between his legs

- ▶ Tori grabs uke's left arm, pulls it towards himself and wraps right leg around uke's neck.
- ▶ Tori turns to his left side and finishes the juji-gatame.

Juji-gatame, uke is on all fours, tori rolls over on his back (pictures 1–3) or on his stomach (picture 4)

Juji-gatame rolling over, uke on all fours, right hand grip, throwing to right shoulder

- ▶ Tori controls uke's right arm with his right hand by grabbing his own left lapel.
- ▶ Tori moves his left foot next to his right foot under uke's chin.
- ▶ Tori throws himself onto his right shoulder, pulling uke with him.
- ▶ Uke rolls onto his back and tori finishes with a juji-gatame.

Juji-gatame with a roll, uke on all fours, left hand grip tori throwing to left side

- ▶ Tori controls uke's right arm with his left hand by grabbing his right lapel.
- ▶ Tori throws himself to the left side with his right foot tucked under uke's body and his left leg controlling uke's head.
- ▶ Tori grabs with his right hand uke's left trouser leg and pulls uke over himself.
- ▶ Tori finishes with a juji-gatame.

Combination tai-otoshi – juji-gatame (also from many other throws, e.g. de-ashi-harai)

- ▶ Tori moves to juji-gatame immediately, controlling uke continuously so that uke does not have time to pull his hand away or turn on his stomach.

Combination yoko-tomoe-nage – juji-gatame

- ▶ Uke blocks yoko-tomoe-nage. Tori turns to the right and moves his left leg to uke's neck, bringing uke down on his back. Tori finishes the juji-gatame.

Combination yoko-tomoe-nage – juji-gatame (side)

- ▶ Uke counters yoko-tomoe-nage by moving to the left.
- ▶ Tori turns to the left and moves his left foot under uke's chin.
- ▶ Tori turns sideways and finishes with juji-gatame.

Combination kami-shiho-gatame – juji-gatame

- ▶ Uke is escaping from kami-shiho-gatame by turning left with his right hand
  ahead. Tori grabs uke's right hand and moves into juji-gatame.

Combination kesa-gatame – juji-gatame

- ▶ Uke is escaping from kesa-gatame by turning left with his right hand ahead.
  Tori grabs uke's right hand and moves into juji-gatame.

SHIME-WAZA

NAMI-JUJI-JIME · GYAKU-JUJI-JIME
MOROTE-JIME/RYO-TE-JIME · TSUKKOMI-JIME · KATATE-JIME
HADAKA-JIME · JIGOKU-JIME · ASHI-JIME
SODE-GURUMA-JIME · KATA-JUJI-JIME · OKURI-ERI-JIME
KOSHI-JIME · KATA-HA-JIME · SANKAKU-JIME

SHIME-WAZA – CHOKES

- ▶ Strangulations are made to the opponent's trachea, the blood vessels in the neck, or jointly to the trachea and the carotid artery/vein.
- ▶ Strangulations require complete control of the uke and close contact.

NAMI-JUJI-JIME – normal cross lock

Backs of the hands crossed upward the

GYAKU-JUJI-JIME – reverse cross lock

Backs of the hands crossed downward

MOROTE-JIME – two-hand choke, hands symmetrical

Tori presses the neck with knuckles

TSUKKOMI-JIME – thrust choke

Tori pulls with his left hand and pushes with his right hand

KATATE-JIME – one hand choke

Tori applies pressure to the carotid artery and trachea

HADAKA-JIME – naked lock (1)

Tori presses the trachea with his wrist

HADAKA-JIME

Uke from the side of the head (2)   Uke on all fours (3)

▶ Tori presses on uke's trachea and pushes uke down on his stomach with his hands and feet.

JIGOKU-JIME – hell's choke, uke on all fours

▶ Tori hooks uke's left arm with his left leg, traps uke's right arm under his armpit with his right hand and moves his left hand to uke's neck. Tori rolls forward, taking uke with him. Tori's left hand completes the jigoku-jime.

ASHI-JIME – leg choke

▶ Uke tries to escape from a hold down, for example. Tori straightens his body on top of uke and pushes with his left leg uke's head from behind his neck. Tori's left hand presses on uke's neck and throat.

▶ Uke is on his back. Tori is on top of uke with one or both leg between uke's legs, or is in kesa-gatame, for example. Tori puts his head next to uke's head and places his left hand under uke's neck, close to uke's ear. With his left hand, tori takes his right hand by the cuff and places his right hand on uke's throat and presses down on the hand, using the cuff as a fulcrum.

SODE-GURUMA-JIME – tori lying on his back on the mat (2)

   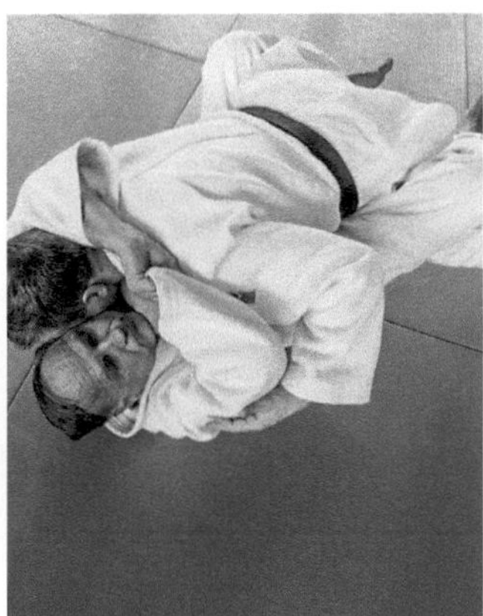

▶ Tori's hands behind uke's neck.

KATA-JUJI-JIME – half-cross lock (1)

   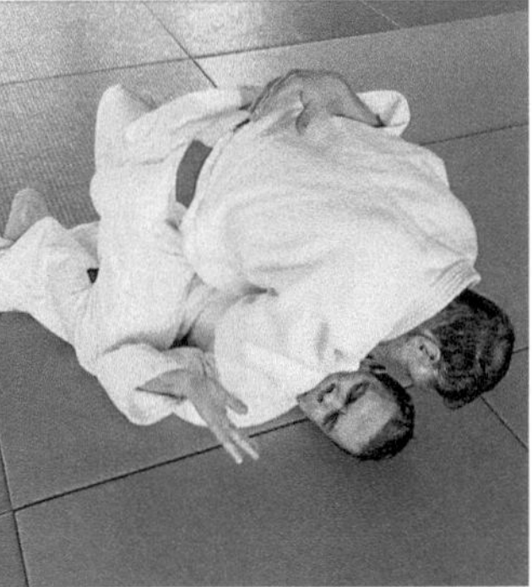

▶ Tori's left hand is palm down on uke's left collar under uke's right hand. Tori's right hand palm up on uke's right lapel.

KATA-JUJI-JIME from the side, uke on all fours (2)

   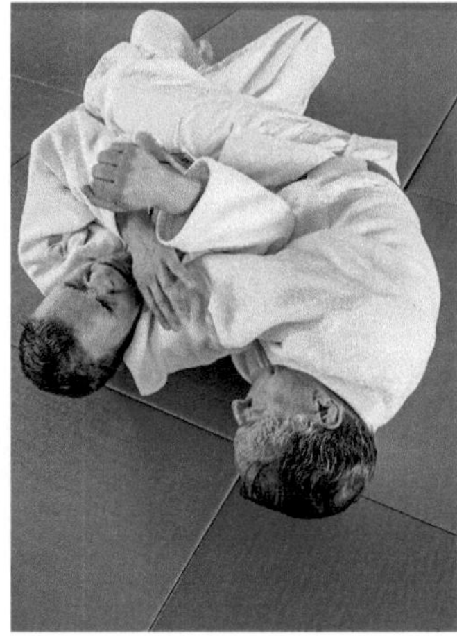

▶ Tori grasps with his left hand under uke's right arm from his left lapel. Right hand grabs uke's judogi by the neck. Tori throws himself on his right side and finishes the choke.

KATA-JUJI-JIME – tori on his back (3)

  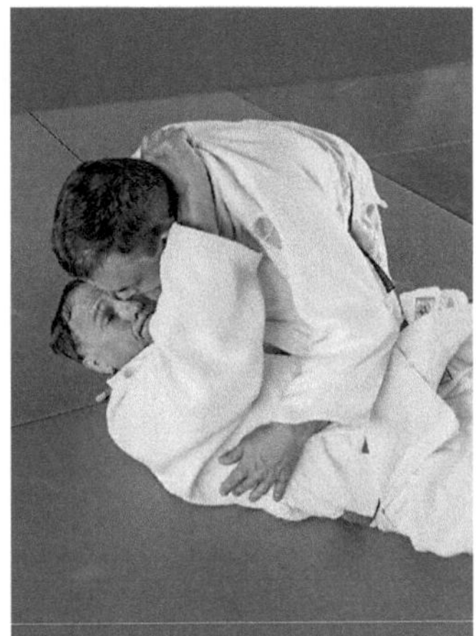 

▶ Uke is on tori's side, for example, trying to get a hold down. Uke's hands are parallel on tori's lapel. One palm is down and the other palm is up. Tori turns his body to the right, thus crossing his arms. Tori finishes with a kata-juji-jime.

KATA-JUJI-JIME – uke on his back (4)

▶ Tori's arms are not crossed at first, one palm facing down and the other facing up. Tori turns his body to the right, thus crossing his arms. Tori finishes with a kata-juji-jime.

KATA-JUJI-JIME – tori on his back (5)

▶ Tori grabs uke's left lapel with left hand, palm down. Tori moves right hand palm up to the right side of uke's head, pushes uke down on his stomach with his feet and finishes with kata-juji-jime.

OKURI-ERI-JIME – sliding collar choke (1)

▶ **1.** Tori takes hold of uke's left lapel with left hand under uke's armpit. **2.** Right hand grasps uke's left collar over his right shoulder, above tori's left hand. **3.** Right hand slides up the collar as high as possible to uke's neck. **4.** Tori moves his left hand up to uke's right lapel and pulls down, and his right hand twists to the right. If tori's right hand is not high enough on uke's neck, okuri-eri-jime fails. Tori may move to kata-ha-jime. See page 175.

OKURI-ERI-JIME – uke on all fours, tori throws himself on his back (2)

  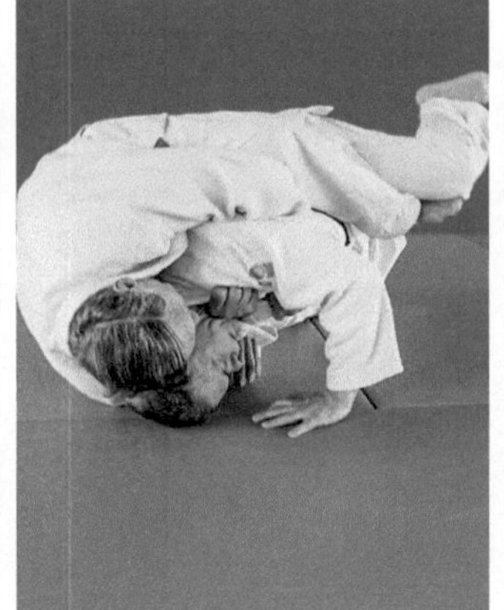 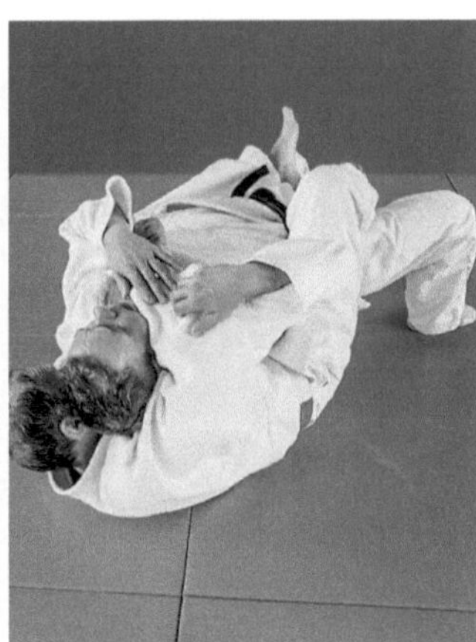

▶ Tori throws himself on his back and uke must follow, which prevents uke from getting up and at the same time the choke is more effective.

OKURI-ERI-JIME – uke on all fours and a tori on his back (3)

▶ Tori starts by pulling uke's left lapel from under his armpit, then places right hand on uke's left lapel, deep underneath his throat. Tori moves his left hand to uke's right collar under his left arm. Tori presses uke down on his stomach with his feet and finishes the okuri-eri-jime.

KOSHI-JIME – hip choke, a variation of okuri-eri-jime

▶ Tori pulls uke forward onto his stomach after uke's failed throw, tori's right hand is under uke's chin in his left collar. Tori controls uke's upper body so that uke cannot roll tori through his left side into the hold down. Tori grabs uke's wrist under his armpit with his left hand, moves his hips next to uke's head and finishes the koshi-jime.

TORI'S LEFT HAND GRIPS FOR KOSHI-JIME

Uke's left wrist   Elbow on uke's neck   On uke's trouser leg

KATA-HA-JIME – single wing choke (1)

▶ Tori's right hand grabs uke's left collar under his chin. Tori's left hand comes under uke's left hand, lifts up uke's left hand and moves behind uke's neck with fingers straight under tori's right arm. As tori breaks uke's balance to the back, tori twists himself to the right and uke is strangled.

KATA-HA-JIME – uke on all fours (2)

   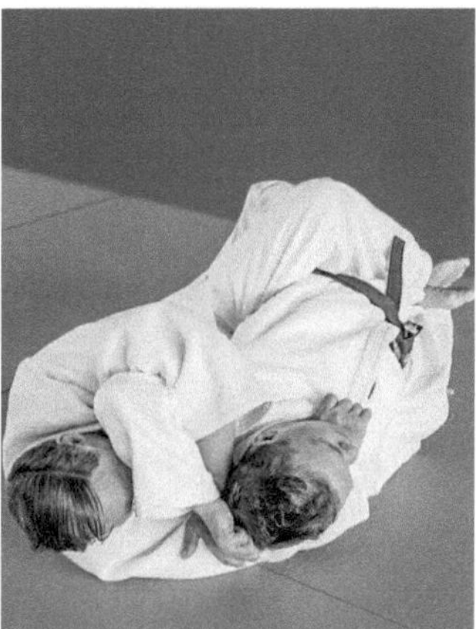

Tori throws himself on his back, pulling uke with him, strengthening at the same time the choke.

SANKAKU-JIME – triangle choke (1)

▶ A choke commonly used in competitions, from which you can move on to armlocks or hold downs. Uke is between tori's legs. Tori controls uke's right arm. Tori puts his right ankle in the knee bend of his left leg around uke's neck, with uke's right arm in between. Tori pulls uke's right arm towards himself while squeezing his legs together.

SANKAKU-JIME – tori lying on his back between uke's legs (2)

▶ Uke tries to get into a hold down from between tori's legs or block sankaku-jime by lifting up. Tori grabs uke's trouser leg with his right hand and by holding uke's head between his legs brings uke onto his back. Tori finishes the sankaku-jime or, depending on the situation, makes a juji-gatame or takes the hold down.

YOKO-SANKAKU-JIME – side triangle bend (3)

▶ Uke is on all fours. Tori places his left leg under uke's right armpit and his right knee on the right side of uke's head. Tori throws himself onto his left side and pulls uke along. The grip is on uke's belt and left elbow. Tori places his left ankle on his right knee bend, ties uke's left hand with the hem of uke's judo-gi to his left hand and finishes the yoko-sankaku-jime by pulling uke's left hand towards himself.

GLOSSARY

A
age – lifting
arashi – storm
ashi – foot
ayumi-ashi – ordinary walking

B
barai – sweep same as harai

D
dan – black belt
de – stepping forward
do – way, principle
dojo – training hall

E
eri – collar

G
gaeshi – counter movement
gake – to hook
garami – to entwine
gari – reaping
gatame – to control
geiko – to exercise
goshi – hip
guruma – wheel
gyaku – opposite

H
ha – wing
hadaka – bare
hajime – referee's opening command
hane – springing
hansoku – breaking the rules
hara – belly
harai – sweep
hidari – left
hiji – elbow
hikikomi – pulling towards oneself
hikite – pulling hand, (sleeve grip)
hishigi – break
hiza – knee

I
ippon – a 10-point performance to end a match

J
jigoku – hell
jigotai – defensive position
jime – choke
ju – flexible
judo – flexible way, sport
judogi – judo suit
judoka – judo practitioner
juji – cross

K
kaeshi – counter-attack

kagari – alternate attack
kami – overhead
kansetsu – joint
kata – formal exercise
kata – shoulder
kata – on one
kataha – one wing
katame-waza – control technique
keiko – drill
ken-ken – jumping
kesa – scarf
Kodokan – original judo teaching location
ko – small
koshi – hip
kubi – neck
kumikata – way to grip
kuruma – wheel
kuzure – variation
kuzushi – breaking one's balance
kyu – student grade

M
maki – wrap
makikomi – wraparound throw to the mat
makura – pillow
mata – inner thigh
mawari – turn around
migi – right
morote – both hands
mune – chest

N
nage-komi – throwing exercise
nami – basic
ne-waza – mat technique

O
o – big, major
obi – belt
okuri – to send
osaekomi – tying
otoshi – drop

R
randori – free practice
rei – bowing
renshu – exercise
renraku – combined, combination
renzoku – combined, combination
ryote – both hands

S

sasae – support
sempai – senior
sensei – teacher
seoi – carry on the back
shiai – competition
shiho – four-way
shime – strangulation
shintai – movement
shisei – stance
shizen-hontai – natural stance
sode – sleeve
soto – outside
sukashi – dodging
sukui – scoop
sumi – corner
sutemi – sacrifice

T

tachi – upright
tai – body
tai-sabaki – turning the body
tandoku-renshu – solo practice
tani – valley
taoshi – take down
tatami – training platform
tate – vertical
tawari – rice bag
te – hand
tobi – jump
tokui – favourite
tori – the person who does the action
tsubame – swallow
tsugi – next
tsukuri – preparation
tsurikomi – lifting pull
tsurite – lifting hand, (collar grip)

U

uchi – inside
uchikomi – repetition training
ude – elbow
uke – receiver of action
ukemi – falling
uki – float
ura – back, reverse
ushiro – back, behind
utsuri – to change, to switch, to switch to another

W

wakare – to separate
waki – armpit
waza – technique
waza-ari – almost completely successful technique

Y

yaku-soku-geiko – pre-arranged exercise
yama-arashi – mountain storm
yoko – side

INDEX

SOURCES

PRINTED

ADAMS, NEIL: Tai-otoshi, Ippon Books LTD., London 1996 (2006)

ANGUS, RON: Competitive Judo, Human Kinetics, 2006

BROUSSAL-DERVAL: La Prépa Physique Judo, 4 trainer Editions, Avril 2012

DAIGO, TOSHIRO: Kodokan Judo Throwing Techniques, Kodansha International Ltd., Tokyo 2005

DEMONTFAUCON, FRÉDÉRIC-WEISS, STÉFANE: Le Grand Livre des Techniques de Judo, Editions Amphora, Fevrier 2011

DRAEGER, DON F-INOKUMA, ISAO: Weight Training for Championship Judo, Kodansha International Ltd, Tokyo

DOUILLET, DAVID: 18 clés pour devenir un champion de la vie, Éditions Michel Lafont, 2001 Neuilly-sur-Seine

L'ESPRIT DU JUDO, JUDO MAGAZINE, LA SOCIÉTÉ K. ÉDITIONS, IVRY-SUR-SEINE 2006–2014

GEESINK, ANTON: My Championship Judo, W. Foulsham & Co. Ltd., London 1966

HOARE, SYD: The A-Z of Judo, Ippon Books Ltd., Bristol 1994 (2006)

HOFMANN, WOLFGANG: Judo: Grundlagen des Stand- und Bodenkampfes, Falken, 1984

INOGAI T.- HABERSETZER R.: Judo Pratique, Éditions Amphora s.a., Paris 2002

INOKUMA, ISAO-SATO, NOBUYUKI: Best Judo, Kodansha International Ltd., Tokyo 1979 (1986)

ISHIKAWA,TAKAHIKO-DRAEGER, DONN: Judo Training Methods, Charles E. Tuttle Publishing Co., Inc.

KANO, JIGORO: Kodokan Judo. Kodansha International Ltd., Tokyo 1986

KASHIWAZAKI, KATSUHIKO: Tomoe-nage, The Crowood Press, Wiltshire 1989

KASHIWAZAKI, KATSUHIKO-NAKANISHI, HIDETOSHI: Attacking Judo, Ippon Books Ltd., London 1995 (2006)

KORPIOLA, KYÖSTI-KORPIOLA, TIMO: Judo Tie mustaan vyöhön (Road to Black Belt), Kustannusosakeyhtiö Tammi., Helsinki 2010

KUDO, KATZUZO: Judo in Action, Throwing Techniques, Japan Publications Trading Co.,Tokyo 1967 (1976)

KUDO, KATZUZO: Judo in Action, Grappling Techniques, Japan Publications Trading Co., Tokyo 1967

LEGGETT T.P-WATANABE, KISABURO: Championships Judo Tai-otoshi and O-uchi-gari Attacks, W. Foulsham & Co Ltd., London 1964

NAKANISHI, HIDETOSHI: Seoi-nage, Ippon Books Ltd., Bristol 1993 (2004)

OHLENKAMP, NEIL: Black Belt, Judo Skills and Techniques, New Holland Publishers Ltd., London 2006

ROUGE, JEAN-LUC: Harai-goshi, Ippon Books Ltd., Bristol 2006

SATO, NOBUYUKI: Ashiwaza, Ippon Books Ltd., Bristol 1992 (2004)

SATO, TETSUYA-OKANO, ISAO: Vital Judo, Japan Publications Inc., Tokyo 1973 (1974)

STARBROOK, DAVE: Judo Starbrook Style, Macdonald and Jane's Publishers Limited., London 1978

SUGAI, HITOSHI: Uchimata, Ippon Books Ltd., London 1991

SWAIN, MICHAEL: Ashiwaza ll, Ippon Books Ltd., Bristol 1994 (2003)

VAN DE WALLE, ROBERT: Pick-Ups, Ippon Books Ltd., Bristol 1993 (2002)

YAMASHITA, YASUHIRO: O-soto-Gari, The Crowood Press Ltd.,Wiltshire 1991

DVD

Adams, Le Gokyo,Fighting Films., Bristol, UK

Adams et Briggs, Judo de competition,
    Fighting Films., Bristol, UK

The Grappling Series, Fighting Films., Bristol, UK

Huizinga, Total Judo, Fighting Films., Bristol, UK

2010 IJF World Circuit,

2010 IJF World Championships,

2011 IJF World Championships,

2013 IJF World Championships,
    Fighting Films., Bristol, UK

Inoue, Uchi-mata

Inoue, Le Samurai

Inoue, Le Judoka Fighting Films., Bristol, UKJeon,
    Le maître coreen, Fighting Films., Bristol, UK

101 Judo Ippons 2006–2008,

101 Judo Ippons 2009–2010,

101 Judo Ippons 2011,

101 Judo Ippons 2012,

303 Classic Judo Ippons Fighting Films., Bristol, UK

Koga, Un Vent Nouveau, Fighting Films., Bristol, UK

Perfectionnement des Ashi-waza,

Perfectionnement des Balayages F.F.J.A./INSEP

Quellmalz, Olympic Judo, Fighting Films., Bristol, UK

22e Stage de Judo de Montpellier-Été 2006, c. 2007

23e Stage de Judo de Montpellier-Été 2007, c. 2008

24e Stage de Judo de Montpellier-Été 2008, c. 2009

25e Stage de Judo de Montpellier-Été 2009, c. 2010

26e Stage de Judo de Montpellier-Été 2010, c. 2011

27e Stage de Judo de Montpellier-Été 2011, c. 2011

28e Stage de Judo de Montpellier-Été 2012, c. 2012

29e Stage de Judo de Montpellier-Été 2013, c. 2013

INTERNET

Finnish Judo Association, www.judo.fi

International Judo Federation www.intjudo.eu

European Judo Union www.eju.net

Author acting as uke for Ichiro Abe in Helsinki in 1964.

Ichiro Abe, 10th dan observes the training of the author and Vesa Riihelä in Helsinki on 30 November 2008. It had been 47 years since Abe first taught at the Vingstedt summer camp in Denmark.

Toshiro Daigo, 10th dan, as a guest in the spring of 1967 in Niko, Japan, with my brother Kyösti, on the left.

The author acting as uke for Anton Geesink, later 10th dan, as a guest at the Turku judo camp in the summer of 1981.

A picture taken by Lasse Holmström in Helsingin Sanomat in 1964 of a Finland-Sweden national match, where the author, aged 19, manages to surprise the multiple Swedish champion Sasse Alsen with an uchi-mata-sukashi.

The author's de-ashi-harai against Gynter Hellberg in a Finland-Sweden match in 1964.

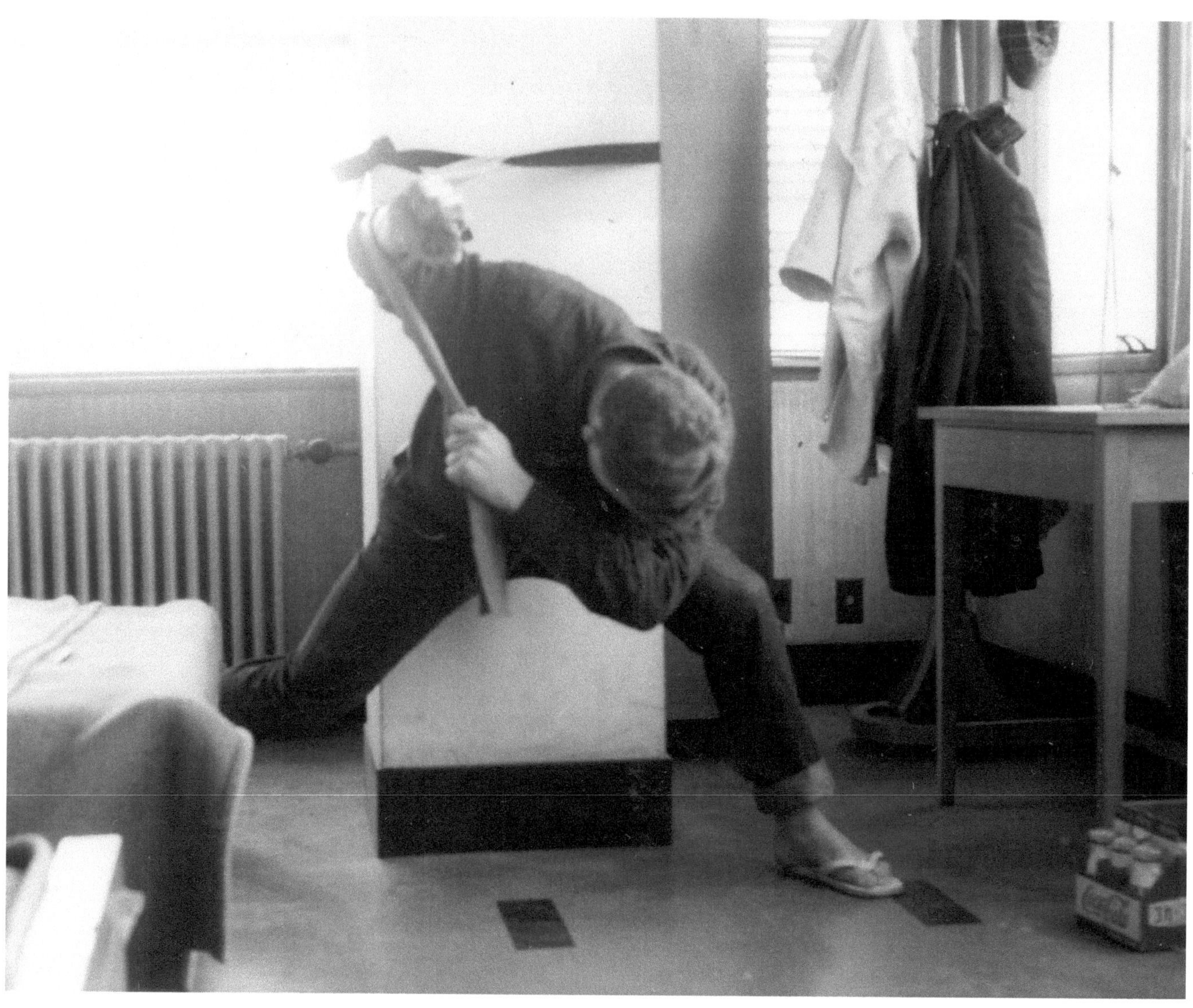

The author's daily isometric tai-otoshi training at the Kodokan dormitory in 1967.

Arttu Laitinen and Peter Mickelsson, the book's assistant and photographer, after a successful kata competition in 2013.